Tithe and Agrarian History from the Fourteenth to the Nineteenth Centuries

An essay in comparative history

Tithe and Agrarian History from the Fourteenth to the Nineteenth Centuries

An essay in comparative history

EMMANUEL LE ROY LADURIE

JOSEPH GOY

TRANSLATED BY SUSAN BURKE

CAMBRIDGE UNIVERSITY PRESS

Cambridge

London   New York   New Rochelle   Melbourne   Sydney

EDITIONS DE
LA MAISON DES SCIENCES DE
L'HOMME

Paris

Published by the Press Syndicate of the University of Cambridge
The Pitt Building, Trumpington Street, Cambridge CB2 1RP
32 East 57th Street, New York, NY 10022, USA
296 Beaconsfield Parade, Middle Park, Melbourne 3206, Australia
and Editions de la Maison des Sciences de l'Homme
54 Boulevard Raspail, 75270 Paris Cedex 06

First published 1982

Printed in Great Britain by
REDWOOD BURN LIMITED
Trowbridge, Wiltshire

Library of Congress Catalogue Card Number: 81–7725

British Library Cataloguing in Publication Data

Le Roy Ladurie, Emmanuel
Tithe and agrarian history from the fourteenth
to the nineteenth centuries
1. Tithes – France – History
I. Title II. Goy, Joseph
254'.8   HJ2287.J/
ISBN 0 521 23974 5

Contents

mυmυmυmυmυmυmυmυmυmυmυmυmυmυmυmυmυmυmυmυmυmυmυmυmυmυmυmυmυmυmυmυmυmυmυmυmυmυmυmυn

List of figures		*page* vii
Preface		ix

Part I: Methodology
by JOSEPH GOY

1	The tithe: an old source for new research	3
	Appendix: List of contributions to the 1977 Paris conference in preparation for the Seventh International Economic History Congress	9
2	The tithe in France and elsewhere	14
3	Methodology	24
4	Towards another kind of history of the tithe, production and productivity	61

Part II: Comparative study of trends
by EMMANUEL LE ROY LADURIE
(*with the collaboration of Marie-Jeanne Tits-Dieuaide*)

5	The end of the Middle Ages: the work of Guy Bois and Hugues Neveux	71
6	The recovery of the sixteenth century	93
7	The seventeenth century: general crisis or stabilization?	120
8	The eighteenth century: economic take-off?	154

Notes	193
References	205

Figures

1 The wheat tithe of the Chapter of Saint-Trophime at Arles, 1660–1789   *page* 38

2 Mediterranean tithe index, 1530–1789 (Goy and Head-Koenig)   48

3 Tithe and *terrage* in the Cambrésis, 1320–1630 (Neveux)   82

4 Wine and grain production in Rust, Hungary, 1630–1850 (Makkai and Zimanyi)   94

5 Grain tithes in south-western Brabant, 1400–1770 (Daelemans in Van der Wee (1978))   96

6 Development of the gross agricultural product in the Spanish Basque country, 1537–1850 (Bilbao and de Pinedo)   113

7 Grain tithes and yield ratios for the Zurich area, 1530–1800 (Head-Koenig)   134

8 Wine production in Anjou, 1550–1790 (Garnier)   141

9 Income from eight wheat tithes paid to the church of Saint-Géry in Cambrai, 1600–1790 (Neveux)   146

10 Agricultural production in Italian Piedmont, 1746–97 (Davico)   163

11 Grain tithes in Galicia, 1600–1837 (Eiras Roel)   170

12 Grain tithes and income from land belonging to the Abbey of Tibaes, Portugal, 1683–1813 (derived from data made available by A. de Oliveira)   173

Figures

13   Rates of rents paid in wheat in the vicinity of
Caen, Normandy, 1630–1790 (derived from
data made available by J. M. Pavard)   180

14   Global and regional income, expressed in
wheat, of the 'Langue de Provence' (estates of
the Knights of St John), 1640–1790 (derived
from data made available by G. Gangneux)   183

15   Grain tithes in the vicinity of Vannes, Brittany,
1628–1785 (Le Goff)   185

The graphs are reproduced by permission of the authors named. Figure 5 is reprinted by permission of Louvain University Press. Figures 4, 6–8, 10–15, copyright Service des Publications, Ecole des Hautes Etudes en Sciences Sociales, Paris; versions of these graphs will appear in *Actes du Colloque préparatoire*.

Preface

The present volume aims at describing, for the English-speaking public, the present state of research on the tithe. This kind of payment, typical of the agrarian *ancien régime*, is of great value for historians because it serves as a rough indicator of changes in the agricultural product (grain, wine etc.) from year to year, decade to decade, or over longer periods. This assertion is true in essence for traditional societies, such as France before 1789, and other countries of Europe and Latin America in the nineteenth century.

The tithe, however, is inseparable from a whole series of other revenues which came from the land and filled, in theory at least, the coffers and the barns of the great landowners, whether they were members of the clergy, the nobility or the upper bourgeoisie. Consequently, we have not separated the tithes (our main preoccupation) from the other revenues derived from the land (rents, seigneurial dues etc.).

This book is divided into two parts. The first part, by Joseph Goy, deals with methodology. The second part is by Emmanuel Le Roy Ladurie with the collaboration of Marie-Jeanne Tits-Dieuaide; this portion deals with long term fluctuations in the product of the tithe and other revenues from the fourteenth to the nineteenth centuries. It is a work of comparative history, focussed on Europe but touching on America, and draws upon the research of nearly a hundred historians from many countries, to whom we are most grateful. Without their patient and brilliant work this book would have been inconceivable.*

* For a list of these historians, see the Appendix to Chapter 1, p. 9

PART ONE

Methodology

JOSEPH GOY

mʊmʊmʊmʊmʊmʊmʊmʊmʊmʊmʊmʊmʊmʊmʊmʊmʊmʊmʊmʊmʊmʊmʊmʊmʊmʊmʊmʊmʊmʊmʊmʊmʊmʊmʊn

The tithe: an old source for new research

Historiography

In Autumn 1963 the Centre National de la Recherche Scientifique (CNRS) recommended, on the advice of Ernest Labrousse, that systematic research be undertaken on the fluctuations in agricultural production during the French *ancien régime*, on the basis of such sources as estate accounts, leases, tithe registers and the contracts made with tithe collectors. Labrousse made this suggestion because he wanted to draw the attention of economic historians to a type of source which a few bold spirits had exploited in an attempt to calculate the relationship between population, production, revenue and consumption, as precisely as possible and preferably over the long term. At this point, important progress was being made in historical demography, thanks to the work of Pierre Goubert on the Beauvaisis, and the research directed by Pierre Chaunu, Louis Henry and Marcel Reinhard, not to mention the iconoclastic hypotheses formulated by René Baehrel in his study of Provence. The 'new rural history' of early modern France had much more to say about the landscape, the agrarian systems, the social structure and prices than about yields, productivity and, above all, production. Two works which appeared more or less simultaneously were crucial in the evolution of ideas about French rural society in the early modern period. Goubert's book, published in 1960,[1] inaugurated a brilliant series of theses which dealt, within the framework of a single region, with complex and fascinating problems concerning demography, social mobility,

social cohesion and social conflict in town and countryside, with the new ambition of studying 'the real life of all
the people'[2] and with 'special sympathy for the small peasants and the badly paid workers'.

At virtually the same time as Goubert, Baehrel (whose
study was published in 1961)[3] used different methods,
methods of quantitative and serial history, to answer
similar questions about the mechanisms, the rhythms and
the cost of economic growth and social change for a rural
society in the preindustrial world. In order to analyse price
changes, Baehrel tried to discover the relative importance
of demand (population and purchasing power) and supply,
i.e. production. He was the first to make a serious study of
a series of tithe figures, which he checked against the production figures for two estates in the countryside near
Arles. Working on tithes paid in money or in kind, farmed
out or collected directly (see below, p. 30), he attempted
to arrive at the percentage of the harvest that they represented in order to calculate long-term production trends
over a period of more than two centuries. Baehrel's methodology was not refined, but his achievement was to
exhume a somewhat neglected source which he treated as
an indicator of changes in agricultural production, a source
which is all the more valuable for being widely found.

A few years later, in 1966, Emmanuel Le Roy Ladurie's
Peasants of Languedoc[4] confirmed the value of the tithe,
both as an indicator of trends in production and as an
index of certain revenues. Henceforward tithes joined
population, prices, wages and incomes as part of the framework of research. The same year the Association Française
des Historiens Économistes reiterated the recommenda-
tions of the CNRS. The Centre de Recherches Historiques
in the Sixth Section of the Ecole Pratique des Hautes Etudes
was charged with studying changes in agricultural production from the fifteenth to the eighteenth centuries as refracted through the tithe documents. Thanks to the
collaboration of a team of historians, some twenty case

studies were prepared and presented at the first Congrès National des Historiens Economistes Français in Paris on 11 and 12 January 1969. Their findings were published under the title *Les fluctuations du produit de la dîme.*[5] Most of these case studies were concerned with France, but the studies of Andalusia and Sicily already represented an attempt to extend the geographical scope of enquiry. These studies provoked a lively, wide-ranging and often polemical discussion of the value of this source and the ways in which it should be used.[6] They succeeded in focussing attention on a mass of archival information previously exploited only by ecclesiastical and institutional historians. They also succeeded in confirming regional variations in the income and the obligations of the peasants in different provinces of France during the *ancien régime*.

While this national study was going on (between 1966 and 1969), Michel Morineau produced his work – which he intended to be controversial – on the misleading appearances of take-off by the French economy in the eighteenth century.[7] He drew on a very important body of statistical and demographic data, and made the tithe series of Onnaing and Quarouble the focal point of this argument. Data drawn from tithes and from agricultural yields and income enabled him to question the existence of an agricultural revolution in France at the end of the *ancien régime*, placing it instead more generally in the first third of the nineteenth century.

For the same area – the north of France – Pierre Deyon collected a large quantity of tithe data in order to study changes in leases by the Hôtel-Dieu at Amiens, and, more generally, trends in rents in Picardy from the sixteenth to the eighteenth centuries.[8]

In other countries historians were showing a similar interest in tithe documents (though perhaps less systematically), and this was to open up very interesting areas for comparative studies. In an article about the Meuse area of Belgium in *Annales* in 1964, J. Ruwet identified some of the conditions necessary for the use of this type of source in the measuring of agricultural production in the *ancien régime*.[9] Also during the 1960s in Hungary, Istvan Kiss collected a vast amount of data from the tithe registers of the sixteenth century, and, together with other Hungarian historians, began an important study of cereal production in the seventeenth and eighteenth centuries in which he incorporated tithe data.[10]

It was above all in Spain, however, that the real pioneer work was undertaken. The earliest of these studies was that of Angel Cabo Alonso, which appeared in 1955.[11] From 1965 on, studies of this type increased, influenced by the work of Gonzalo Anes, and in particular by his book on agrarian crises in modern Spain.[12]

Although the opening up of all these fields of research made it possible to draw comparisons on a European scale, it was still necessary to find a suitable framework in which this kind of comparison could take place. Once again it was Labrousse who, on the occasion of a conference on historical method organized by A. Eiral Roel at the University of Santiago de Compostela in 1973, suggested reviving the French enquiry of 1966–9.[13] After this conference, dedicated to the discussion of research on the fluctuations in the tithe product, it was agreed to launch an international enquiry entitled 'Peasant dues, tithes and trends in agricultural production in preindustrial societies'.[14] Le Roy Ladurie and I were made responsible for this study. We wanted this survey to cover a very wide geographical area and a very long time span. More than sixty researchers from seventeen countries agreed to participate, and met in Paris (30 June–2 July 1977) for a conference in preparation for the Seventh International Economic History Congress.[15]

As the list of authors and subjects indicates, this new project spanned six centuries, from the fourteenth to the nineteenth, and above all, it considerably extended the geographical area previously covered by research. Eastern,

The tithe: an old source for new research

Western, Central and Southern Europe are all well represented by contributions on the following countries: Eire, Great Britain, Belgium, Holland, West Germany, East Germany, Switzerland, Hungary, Poland, the USSR, Italy, Spain and Portugal. Research on Quebec, Mexico and on Chile (undertaken by Marcello Carmagnani a few years ago)[16] has provided us with some very interesting points of comparison with regard to the nature of the sources, ways of using them and general trends. Finally, as for France (the subject of most of the studies at the 1969 conference), a serious gap is now being filled by research in Brittany and the area west of the Paris Basin. In the following chapters I shall return to the other problems considered at this preparatory conference, problems concerning the diversity of sources, sophistication of methods and widening of the range of questions asked.

This entire study will be published shortly by the Ecole des Hautes Etudes and the CNRS, but it is already possible to consult the *Proceedings of the Seventh International Economic History Congress*, edited by Michael Flinn.[17] Volume I contains an introduction by Le Roy Ladurie and myself,[18] and the five national reports presented in Edinburgh in August 1978:

H. Van der Wee (Louvain), Agrarian development in the Low Countries as reflected in tithe and rent statistics, 1250–1800.

M. Aymard (Ecole des Hautes Etudes) and G. L. Basini (Parma), Agricultural production and productivity in Italy (16th–18th centuries).

L. Makkai (Budapest), Peasant dues, tithes, rents and trends in agricultural production during the preindustrial era in some Eastern European countries.

A. L. Head-Koenig (Geneva), The measurement of production and cereal yields in Germany and Switzerland in the modern period.

G. Anes and A. Garcia Sanz (Madrid), Tithes and agricultural production in modern Spain.[19]

Methodology

For the Netherlands, North and South, the report mentioned above, together with nine studies on the tithe, rents, yields, productivity and the problem of the 'agricultural revolution', were collected in a volume entitled *Productivity of Land and Agricultural Innovation in the Low Countries (1250–1800)* by Van der Wee and Van Cauwenberghe,[20] who participated in both the preparatory conference in Paris and the Edinburgh Congress.

Another team, led by Verhulst and Vandenbroecke (Ghent), has just published a collection of essays on agricultural productivity in Flanders and Brabant, from the fourteenth to the nineteenth centuries[21] which draw on tithe data. These two collections mean that the Netherlands, North and South, is one of the best documented areas in Western Europe.

We could almost say the same for the Iberian Peninsula, if all the work in hand was actually published. We already have access to some important studies, which include Baudilio Barreiro Mallon on the Xallas region of Galicia in the eighteenth century,[22] and Manuel Garzon Pareja on the establishment and abolition of the tithe in the diocese of Granada.[23] Apart from the work of Gonzalo Anes which we have already mentioned, the most important of these studies are Pinedo's work on economic growth and social change in the Basque country,[24] Angel Garcia Sanz's analysis of development and crises in Old Castille during the *ancien régime*,[25] and M. A. Ladero Quesada and M. Gonzalez Jimenez's work on the production, commercialization and consumption of cereals in the Kingdom of Seville in the fifteenth century.[26]

All in all a wonderful harvest of tithe data over the last twenty years! Not only, to borrow Labrousse's phrase, did the study of production 'take off' simultaneously in several countries, but comparative studies on a wide, international scale are now possible, thanks to the use of a source which has always been known but was previously used only for the history of the Church or administration. By its very

8

nature the tithe is one of the best means of measuring trends in agricultural production: its fundamental characteristics, like the variety of forms it took, account for the methodology we have suggested.

Appendix

Contributions to the conference held in Paris (30 June–2 July 1977) in preparation for the Seventh International Economic History Congress.

West Germany
W. Achilles (Göttingen), The development of the income of the peasants in lower Saxony during the last third of the 18th century.

F. W. Henning (Cologne), Die Entwicklung der Dienste und der Abgaben im 16. Jahrhundert in Mitteleuropa.

East Germany
H. H. Muller (Berlin), Le mouvement des prestations paysannes, des rentes et de la production agricole dans la Marche du Brandenbourg, du XVe au XVIIIe siècle (quelques seigneuries).

Eire
D. Dickson (Dublin), Tithe and rent as sources for Irish agricultural trends before 1815.

Great Britain
R. Kain (Exeter), Les dîmes, les relevés de dîmes et la mesure de la production agricole dans la Grande-Bretagne préindustrielle.

P. K. O'Brien and D. Heath (Oxford), The efficiency of British and French agriculture, 1815–1914.

Belgium
M. Gutman (Texas), War, tithe and agricultural production: the Meuse Basin north of Liège: 1661–1740.

M. J. Tits-Dieuaide (Paris), Rendements céréaliers dans les environs de Louvain, 1404–1726.

E. Van Cauwenberghe and H. Van der Wee (Louvain), Productivité, évolution du prix d'affermage et superficie de l'entreprise agricole aux Pays-Bas du XIVe au XVIIIe siècle.

Spain

G. Anes Alvarez (Madrid), Las fluctuaciones de la producción agricola durante el siglo XVIII y comienzos del XIX en Espana.

R. Benitez Sanchez-Blanco (Valencia), Diezmos andaluces: series malaguenas de diezmos del trigo.

L. M. Bilbao and E. F. de Pinedo (Bilbao). Evolución del producto agricola bruto en el Pais Vasco peninsular, 1537–1850. Primeira aproximación a traves de los diezmos y de la primicia.

J. Casey (East Anglia), Structure et développement de l'agriculture de Valence à l'époque moderne, 1500–1700.

A. Eiras Roel (Santiago), Dîme et mouvement du produit agricole en Galice (1600–1837).

A. Garcia Lombardo Vinas (Santiago), Formas de apropriación del excedente agrario en una economia senorial: las rentas forales y el derecho de la luctuosa en la Galicia del antiguo regimen.

A. Garcia Sanz (Madrid), La producción de cereales y leguminosas en Castilla la vieja: los diezmos del obispado de Segovia de 1570 a 1800.

M. Garzon Pareja (Granada) and B. Vincent (CNRS–CRH, Paris), Tributos campesinos a la Iglesia en el Reino de Granada.

M. Lemeunier (Casa de Velasquez), Approche méthodologique des dîmes de Murcie à l'époque moderne.

J. M. Palop Ramos (Valencia), El producto diezmal valenciano durante los siglos XVII y XVIII. Aproximación a su estudio.

J. M. Palop Ramos and R. Benitez Sanchez-Blanco (Valencia), Evolución de la renta fenda valenciana en el siglo XVIII.

P. Ponsot (Lyon II), Malthus n'était-il pas prophète en Andalousie? Les rendements des céréales en Basse-Andalousie du XVIIe au XIXe siècle.

B. Vincent (CNRS–CRH, Paris), Mesures de la production dans le royaume de Grenade au XVIe siècle.

Appendix

France

G. Beaur (Paris), Le mouvement annuel de la rente foncière chartraine, 1760–1780.

G. Bois (Besançon), Sur les mouvements de longue durée en économie féodale.

P. Butel (Bordeaux), Production viticole et rente foncière en Bordelais au XVIIIe siècle.

C. Chereau (Brussels), Pour une approche méthodique des baux angevins et manceaux aux XVIIe et XVIIIe siècles.

J. M. Constant (Paris), L'évolution de la rente foncière et de la rentabilité de la terre en Beauce aux XVIe et XVIIe siècles.

L. Gangneux (Grenoble), Biens et seigneuries de l'ordre de Malte en France méridionale aux XVIIe et XVIIIe siècles: problèmes de production et de productivité agraires.

J. Garnier (Caen), Eléments de conjoncture: production et rente foncière en Normandie, Maine et Anjou.

J. Georgelin (Marseille-Luminy), L'écologie du froment en Europe occidentale.

T. Le Goff (Toronto), Autour de quelques dîmes vannetaises (XVIIe–XVIIIe siècle).

M.Th. Lorcin (Lyon II), La fraude des décimables: mouvement court ou mouvement long?

L. Michel (Montreal), Quelques données sur le mouvement de la rente foncière en Anjou, du milieu du XVIIe siècle à la Révolution.

M. Morineau (Clermont-Ferrand), Cambrésis et Hainaut: des frères ennemis?

M. Morineau (Clermont-Ferrand), La dîme et le zeste, XIVe–XXe siècles.

J. Nicolas (Montpellier), L'enjeu décimal dans l'espace rural savoyard.

J. P. Pavard (Caen), Le mouvement de la rente foncière dans la plaine de Caen d'après trois échantillons. Fin XVIe siècle–1789. Bilan provisoire.

A. Poitrineau (Clermont-Ferrand), Productions animales et végétales dans les montagnes d'Auvergne au XVIIIe siècle.

Holland

A. M. Van der Woude (Wageningen), The secular movement of rent for pasture-land in North-Holland and the problem of profitability in agriculture, 1570–1800.

Hungary
I. Hunyadi (Strasbourg), Production agricole dans le diocèse de Györ au XVIe siècle. Bilan provisoire.

I. Kiss (Budapest), Volume et production des exploitations paysannes en Hongrie, XVIe–XVIIIe siècles. Base démographique et capacité d'alimentation.

L. Makkai and V. Zimanyi, with the collaboration of P. Ban and Mme Janokine Ujvary (Budapest), Les registres de dîme comme sources de l'histoire de la production agricole en Hongrie dans la période du féodalisme tardif, 1500–1848.

Italy
B. Anatra (Cagliari), Cenni sulla produzione agricola nella Sardegna barocca.

M. Aymard (EHESS), Production et productivité agricoles: l'Italie du Sud à l'époque moderne.

L. Basini (Parma), Produzione agricola e redditi agrari nelle regioni agricole dell'Italia settentrionale (XVI–XVII).

O. Cancila (Palermo), Sulla rendita fondiaria in Sicilia della fine del Quattrocento all'Unità d'Italia.

R. Davico (Turin), Les gabelles sur la production et la consommation en Sicile (fin XVIe–début XVIIe). La production agricole en Piémont entre 1739 et 1799.

F. Landi (Bologne), L'exploitation des paysans et l'organisation productive dans les grandes propriétés ecclésiastiques du territoire de Ravenne au XVIIIe siècle.

J. Revel (CNRS–CRH, Paris), Rendements, productivité et production agricoles; le cas du grand domaine en Italie centrale aux XVIIe-XVIIIe siècles.

M. A. Visceglia, Rente féodale et agriculture dans Les Pouilles à l'époque moderne, XVIe–XVIIIe siècles.

Mexico
C. Morin (Montreal), Le mouvement du produit décimal et l'évolution des rapports fonciers au Mexique du XVIIe au XIXe siècle.

Quebec
J. P. Wallot et G. Paquet (Montreal and Ottawa), Rentes foncières, dîmes et revenus paysans. Le cas canadien.

Appendix

Poland
J. Topolski (Poznan) and A. Wyczanski (Warsaw), Les fluc-
tuations de la production agricole en Pologne aux XVIe–
XVIIe siècles.

Portugal
A. de Araujo Oliveira (Lisbon), Prestations paysannes,
dîmes, rente foncière et mouvement de la production
agricole à l'époque préindustrielle dans le pays du Nord-
Ouest portugais, 1626–1821.

Switzerland
A. L. Head-Koenig (Geneva), Les fluctuations des rendements et du produit décimal céréaliers dans quelques
régions du plateau suisse, 1560–1800.

Ch. Pfister (Berne), An analysis of fluctuations in tithe
curves based on Swiss data within the period 1687–
1796.*

USSR
J. Kahk, H. Ligi and E. Tarvel (Estonia), A parallel study of
agricultural production and feudal duties of the
peasantry in Estonia in the 16th to the 19th centuries.

USA
V. Burton (Illinois), The development of tenantry and the
post-bellum afro-american social structure in Edgefields
County, South Carolina.

---

* Published under the title 'Climate and economy in eighteenth century
Switzerland', *Journal of Interdisciplinary History* IX.2(1978).

2

The tithe in France and elsewhere

The form of the tithe in France under the ancien regime

The tithe as a biblical institution dates back almost 2,000 years and was well established by canon law. It should have been levied on the totality of agricultural products, on livestock, on the proceeds from fishing, hunting and from windmills, as well as on the profits of trade and industry. But in fact it quickly became a traditional means by which the Church could collect each year a percentage of the fruits of the earth, in other words, of crops and livestock. Very roughly, and allowing for the inevitable regional variations, one can distinguish between

(1) the major tithes, which were levied on the basic components of agricultural production, wheat, barley, oats, rye and wine;

(2) the lesser tithes or 'green tithes' on vegetables and fruit from gardens and orchards;

(3) the tithes on livestock, commonly known as 'blood tithes'.[1]

Because the tithe was based on custom rather than on rigid laws it was a living institution liable to change. In addition to the long-established tithes (the *dîmes solites*) others could be introduced, especially on new crops (maize, potatoes etc.). These were the so-called 'exceptional tithes' (*dîmes insolites*) which were often a source of conflict between the tithe collector and the producers. It was in the interests of the latter to prevent these new tithes from being paid continuously for forty years, since this would make them 'long-established' (*solites*) and the amount levied was then increased.[2]

In theory the tithe was levied on all land belonging to the common people, the nobility or the Church, although religious orders such as the Carthusians, the Cistercians, the Cluniacs and certain others were exempt. It did not, however, apply to produce from lakes, wild grasslands and woods. There were enormous local and regional variations in the level of the tithe. It hovered around 10%, but could be as high as 14%, or fall as low as 2.5%; it was also liable to change over time in response to the level of resistance or hostility on the part of the peasants.

Since the tithe represented a percentage of the harvest, it should provide an obvious and extremely useful index of agricultural trends. Unfortunately, our task is complicated by the methods of tithe collection.

Methods of collection and assessment

'God's share' – which is how the tithe was described in canon law – reached the clergy or their substitutes in various forms and by different means.[3] It was quite rare for the peasants themselves to be responsible for collecting and transporting their tithe to the granaries and warehouses of the clergy: this system would, of course, have encouraged the farmers to cheat on both quantity and quality. It was normally those to whom the tithe was due, or their deputies, who were responsible for collecting and checking it. We may distinguish five main ways in which the tithe could be collected:

	Collected directly by clergy	Farmed for a single harvest	Farmed for several harvests
In kind	1	2	4
In money		3	5

Methodology

(1) The tithe could be levied *directly* by the clergy or by their agents. It would be collected each year, as the harvests came in, from the fields, the threshing-floor, the wine-press, the stables or any other place where the crops were stored. This was a directly administered tithe.

(2) The tithe could equally well be farmed out (that is, leased) to one or more persons whom we will call tithe farmers. This agreement could be for *one* or for *several* years (types 2, 3, 4, 5), and it could cover tithes in *kind* (types 2, 4) or in *money* (types 3, 5). The tithe farmer was responsible for collecting the tithe and for handing over to the lessor the sum agreed in the contract. He also had to make a profit, which was his remuneration. If the contract specified tithes to be paid in kind, the farmer paid them in wheat, wine, oil etc. If it specified money, he had to sell all, or part, of the goods collected and pay the lessor out of the proceeds: his own profit then depended on his business ability, on the fluctuation of prices at the time and hence on supply and demand. When the agreement was for only one year, the lease was drawn up just before the harvest of a particular product. This was a fairly crude system, but it protected the interests of both parties. If the lease covered a longer period (two, three, five, six or nine years), given the speculative nature of the enterprise, the tithe was usually very broadly based: it could cover all the crops from the land under consideration and it could also become mingled with the collection of other kinds of income, such as rents or seigneurial dues.

The first type of tithe is to be found in the ecclesiastical accounts in series G or H in the French departmental archives, or the account books collected in miscellaneous manuscript sections of the national or departmental archives. Types 2–5 can be found in series G or H or in the registers of lay notaries (series E) or in ecclesiastical notaries (series II E, G and H). The ideal situation arises:

(a) when one has access to both the tithe register and the

lease. In this case, one source acts as a check on the other, or enables us to fill the gaps that are inevitable in this type of document,

(b) when it is possible to establish continuous series, ideally covering more than one century – series which reveal certain movements or trends which we will discuss later.

French archives often satisfy both conditions and have already yielded veritable treasures for the historian of long-term trends: there is, for example, the long series for Provence (16th–18th centuries) compiled by Baehrel (Baehrel 1961). These cover production trends over periods of thirty years, trends which were first established on the basis of price curves and then confirmed by Goy when he drew up the Mediterranean tithe index.[4] There is also Le Roy Ladurie's mass of tithe data for Languedoc (Le Roy Ladurie 1966), which enabled him to construct the neo-Malthusian model he has put forward for the period from the end of the fifteenth to the middle of the eighteenth centuries. Pierre Deyon produced a fine series for Picardy for the sixteenth to the eighteenth centuries (Deyon n.d.); Michel Morineau has a complete and reliable set for the tithes of Taques d'Onnaing and Quarouble from 1400 to 1789 (Morineau 1970); and Hugues Neveux has collected data for the Cambrésis from the end of the fourteenth century to the beginning of the seventeenth.[5] For the Toulouse area we have Georges Frêche's study of the tithe revenues of the canons of Saint-Sernin at Toulouse,[6] and for Normandy, Guy Bois' series go from 1377 to the middle of the sixteenth century.[7] Jean Nicolas has used this type of source for Savoy, and has given much thought to the various ways of exploiting tithe data.[8] We must not, of course, leave out the papers offered at the first Congrès des Historiens Economistes Français on the Paris region, the Cambrésis, Burgundy, Alsace, the Lyons area, Auvergne and Provence.[9] It is clearly not possible to mention all the series of tithe curves or of contracts studied in France in the last twenty years, and in any case, these have often been considered from a rather different angle from our own.[10]

The international tithe zone and the diversity of sources

As already suggested by research done on Spain, Hungary and Belgium, tithe studies of the kind we are interested in are to be found throughout the Catholic (if not the Christian) world, though they are not all equally reliable.

The preparatory studies[11] for the Seventh International Economic History Congress confirmed the exceptional quality of certain national sources (Hungary and Spain, for example), but they also stressed the importance of drawing on a wide variety of records. Participants in the survey drew on material which was often new and extremely varied – either because there were no tithe series available, or because the records were incomplete or unsuitable.

As far as Hungary is concerned, it appears that the tithe registers did provide the most reliable and the fullest data from which to establish the long-term trends in agricultural production: the data were drawn from both Catholic and Protestant holdings, and referred to wheat, rye, barley, oats, wine, bees and lambs. This tithe was introduced into Hungary in the eleventh century, when the country was converted to Christianity and the Hungarian State was emerging. As in many other countries, the clergy did not manage to establish or control the tithe collection, but very often handed this over to the local *seigneurs*. From the middle of the sixteenth century, however, after the Turks had occupied central Hungary, the tithe became a 'royal tithe' in most counties: this meant that it was leased to the Royal Chamber, thus making it a state tax intended to cover the cost of defence. It is then clear that tithe data in Hungary are valuable for two reasons: they cover a long period of time, and we know exactly how the tithe was col-

lected. We have some incomplete accounts from the thirteenth century, but the real series covers about thirty
counties (or more than 100,000 square kilometres) and
goes up to the middle of the nineteenth century, in other
words, to the abolition of the tithe in 1848. These data are
extremely detailed. In the case of wheat, for example, they
tell us the number of sheaves supplied by each farmer, a
rare piece of information which has opened up new lines of
research into this type of production and productivity. The
tithe can also be studied in conjunction with a parallel obli-
gation, the *nona*, for which we also have records from the
sixteenth century onwards. This was a fine due to the holy
king Stephen by those who had not paid the tithe. In the
fourteenth century it was taken over by the *seigneurs* and it
then took the form of a compulsory levy of 10% of the
harvest to be paid in kind. This meant that the real tithe
was worth less than its theoretical value of 10%. Finally,
historians of Hungary have access to what is virtually a set
of photographs of the economy – the survey of 1707
(Prince Rákoczi's *Dica*), which was a complete census of
households and all their goods and production. It covers all
social classes and was drawn up for the purpose of impos-
ing a tax on the income and profits of each Hungarian aged
sixteen or over.[12]

As Gonzalo Anes and Angel Garcia Sanz reminded us in
their papers at the Edinburgh Congress, documentation for
Spain is also 'one of the richest in the world'.[13] We know
what the peasants paid in nearly every province, thanks to
the *tazmias* books kept by those who collected the tithes, or
were entitled to do so; these books are preserved in the
parish archives. What is more, these data can be checked
against the annual returns found in private, ecclesiastical
or even national archives. The tithe was levied on all
produce from the land and on all properties, except those
of the clergy when these were farmed by the priests themselves; very often the major tithes were to be paid in kind and
the others in money. This situation, for which there is an

exceptional abundance of evidence, was fairly similar to that in most regions of France. But there was a particularly interesting bonus: in certain regions the tithe was divided into roughly three parts: one third went to the bishop and his chapter; another third to the local clergy and the last third was divided between the king and the building fund committee. Not only are there records of accounts for these royal *tercias*, but also for a supplementary tithe, the *excusado*. Exceptionally, then, we have three possible sources of documentation which enable us to fill in any gaps in the tithe series and to compare or check the figures.

It is not surprising to find a similar abundance of archive material for Latin America. This has already been pointed out by Marcello Carmagnani (Carmagnani 1973) and has recently become a focus of attention.[14] In the Spanish colonies the tithe was levied on all agricultural products and livestock, whether cereals, sugar cane, cattle or cheese. It applied to all farmers – even if they were secular clergy or members of religious orders – apart from the native Indians who were not liable to pay tithe on American products grown on their own or communal land. The archives are certainly rich in material, but the system of collection was also very simple: those who were entitled to receive the tithe, or their agents, collected it from each farm or estate. They in turn were obliged to submit detailed and precise accounts in the form of annual reports to the diocesan administration, many of which have been preserved.

On the other hand, we are faced with a serious shortage of tithe data for certain European countries like Italy, Germany or Poland.

In Italy, there are scarcely any long tithe series except for Sardinia and the area around Otranto.[15] Here, for some reason, tithes did not have the importance they usually did in Mediterranean countries. In most cases the tithe cannot be separated from seigneurial dues, rents or even taxes. When it did have an independent existence it was granted to or usurped by laymen; since it was sometimes transformed into a hearth tax or allowed to fall into disuse, or levied on minor products but not on grain, it accounts for only a very small part of the revenues of an extremely rich Church.[16]

The work of Head-Koenig, Veyrassat-Herren and Pfister has shown how rich the Swiss archives are in tithe series for the last quarter of the fifteenth century, and in particular for the Protestant Cantons from the sixteenth century on.[17]

The same cannot be said for Germany. In the Southern States, where the tithe was a major element in the revenue of the clergy, the Church records which have been preserved are far from complete, although we do have some fine, long-term series from the hospitals and universities which to some extent compensate for these gaps. For the Northern States, the situation is even more difficult, since there 'the tithe returns and the seigneurial dues were lumped together, although they may have followed different trends' (Head-Koenig, *Proceedings*, 153. In addition, it is very difficult to assemble long series of these tithes because the data are scattered around various archives.

In the case of Poland, even though there was a tithe system, it is just not possible to undertake the kind of research we are suggesting: either because – so far – no tithe records have been found in either private, Church or State archives; or because the tithe, which was paid first in kind, then in money, took the form of a subscription which was set at a fixed rate for a long period.[18] This makes it necessary to look at other documents, for example the periodic assessments of the income of estates, the revenue from windmills or food consumption records.

A completely different type of source has been used by Kahk, Ligi and Tarvel for Estonia,[19] and by Nossov for Russia.[20] As Kahk pointed out in the discussions at the preliminary conference: 'You have the tithe! We have the *corvée*!' The records of the *corvée*, although they tell us little about agricultural production, are an extremely useful source of information about the changes in the revenue that the landlord drew from his estate, and they help us with the difficult problems of establishing when and how the peasants were enserfed, and in assessing the importance of the *corvée* in the agricultural systems of Eastern Europe. These problems have already been studied intensively by Soviet historians.

Systematic research into tithe documents has clearly shown (1) that this type of source existed, in various forms, in different countries over a wide geographical area, (2) that in certain cases the documents are missing or exist in a form which cannot be used, and (3) that their interpretation necessitates a certain number of precautions and methodological choices, a point which has provoked a lively and important discussion to be considered in the following chapter. These various studies have also led a large number of historians to make use of other sources which can throw light on agricultural production and productivity. In addition to the long series of tithes paid in kind or money, taken from estate accounts or leases and preserved in Church, private or State archives, there is also a place, as we have already seen, for the use of other quantitative data, either by themselves or together with the tithe. These include price series for the main food products, land surveys, port accounts relating to the quantity and prices of commercial goods, taxes on production and consumption, surveys and censuses of households and goods (for example the *Dica* of Prince Rákoczi, and the English *Nonae Inquisitiones*), estate reports, and the measures taken to improve their profits (for example the Portuguese *Estados*, or the *Visites Générales* of the Knights of St John), ground rents in kind or in money taken from parish records or notary registers, and finally, accounts concerning villages, or great estates, and series of data on yields, by the crop or by the acre.[21] This list does not include certain exceptional sources. The records of the Zurich hospital between 1718 and 1786, for example, give us a year by year account of the areas sown, the quantities of grain used and the ensuing yield.[22] The accounts of church estates in Andalusia give three annual figures: the amount harvested, yields (in relation to the seed sown and the surface area covered) and rents.[23] The general tithe census of England in 1836 should enable us to make a map of agriculture in England and Wales in the first third of the nineteenth century.[24] Despite this great wealth of documentary evidence, we have to express one regret: most of our sources refer only to cereal production. We do not have enough comparable series of data for wine production or even livestock. The discussion of methods must therefore be based essentially on cereal production and productivity, with occasional references to the gross agricultural product taken as a whole.

3

Methodology

The tithe as a source

In France, the tithe has traditionally been studied by canon lawyers or historians of institutions, first with the purpose of justifying the tithe or improving the methods of collection (till 1789), and later to estimate the importance of the tithe relative to other dues the peasants of the *ancien régime* were obliged to pay to the State, the Church and the *seigneurs*.[1] For the last twenty years the tithe has been looked at from a radically different angle, and, in the course of the two great national and international surveys and other studies mentioned in the previous chapter, it has become the focus of a new type of research. This is because of the nature of the tithe, because it is possible to constitute long series, sometimes spanning several centuries, and because it enables us to make comparative studies of a very large number of European or non-European countries in the preindustrial period. It is the ambiguous nature of the tithe which makes it so interesting to the historian: it was an integral part of the dues extracted by the ruling class from the gross agricultural product, but it belongs essentially to Quesnay's second category, that of the net product.

If every tithe represents a movement of the net product between those liable to pay and those entitled to receive it, it also represents a proportion (varying locally) of the gross product – in other words of the harvests.

We may consider one or more tithe series over the long

term from three different points of view necessitating three different approaches.

(1) The tithe is, by its nature, a way of measuring the revenue that one sector of the landowning classes – the Church – drew from the producers.

(2) On another level, the tithe can be used to identify and measure general trends in agricultural production. This type of analysis is possible but difficult since tithes may be farmed out; in that case one has to make allowance for rises and falls in production and the consequent fluctuations in the amounts paid to the tithe farmers, and hence to the clergy as lessors. Increases or sudden declines in population and the flexibility of the market must also be taken into account.

(3) On a third level, tithe data make an indispensable contribution to the formulation of hypotheses about the *movement* of agricultural production: in certain privileged cases, where cross-checking is possible, we can be virtually certain of the strength as well as the direction of the movement. The two collective enquiries have produced some very substantial data on ecclesiastical income as a net product, and on overall trends in agricultural production. Even though our enthusiasm was not entirely shared by every member of the group, we were anxious to impose a common strategy on the 1966 survey. As we wrote in *Fluctuations* (Goy and Le Roy Ladurie 1972), 'this survey, covering a wide area, has enabled us to collect a whole series of detailed files on the tithe. All we have done with these is to derive short-term and long-term trends, either copying the figures from the registers or deflating them.[2] In short, it was a question of bringing to light a document; of presenting the phenomenon of the tithe as it revealed itself. This is a positivist and global procedure; it is quite legitimate since we are not claiming to reconstitute the movement of the gross product but merely to identify, for their own sake, the fluctuations over time of a certain type of net product.'

As far as the gross product is concerned, these same files have opened up new areas of research which, as a result of intensive studies and monographs, have enabled us to produce 'an in-depth history of agricultural production'. By studying the amount of tithe paid we have been able to discern trends in agricultural income and in the dues the farmers had to pay, both of which give us clues to agricultural production. It seemed to us

(a) that every genuine tithe was affected by the underlying trends in production, and in this way it *refracted* the gross product. Thus any study of the net product based on the tithe itself provided certain information about trends in the gross product.

(b) that certain tithe series accurately *reflected* trends in the gross product, where the tithe returns were either completely stable over a long period, or in cases where we can work out the fluctuations. Because the tithe is so widespread in time and space, in each of these cases, though in varying degrees, it appears to be a useful and an excellent indicator of one of the elements which allow us to reconstitute trends in the gross and net product.

A similar project, to which we shall return, was set up to examine the leases of farms and estates in areas where there were no tithe series or where, as in the Beauce and the Beauvaisis, the tithe was only one element in a kind of contract which incorporated all sorts of goods and rights. This is not ideal but it enables us (very crudely for the short and medium term, but more successfully in the long term) to fill the gaps in tithe records.[3]

The question of tithe fraud

The least serious argument put forward by some historians against the use of tithe documents is that the figures may have been distorted by fraud. We are by no means denying that this may have happened: although the tithe was 'to be collected and not delivered' except in rare cases, and although the peasant was not allowed to do his harvesting before the tithe collector had inspected it, all the documents indicate that fraud was a problem. When, in addition to recording the bare figures, collectors or clerks describe the methods of collecting, measuring and transporting the tithe, they frequently mention the 1,001 ruses devised by the peasants, always reluctant to pay this due. Cheating on the tithe is as old as the tithe itself and has been studied from every angle in the Lyonnais,[4] in Auch[5] and in Savoy.[6] It was a universal practice to put aside some sheaves of wheat or some bunches of grapes before the collector's visit; to try to deceive him by placing some of the grain in a hiding place carefully chosen in advance, bringing the sheaves in from the fields under the pretext of bad weather or simply 'misunderstanding' the date of the collector's visit. It is also quite clear that throughout our period, roughly from the fourteenth to the eighteenth century, the collectors steadily lost out. In many areas of France the tithe levels fell and the reimposition of liability in certain cases which had been exempt and the introduction of a higher level of tithe (a ninth instead of a tenth part) by no means succeeded in slowing down this erosion of income. As Marie-Thérèse Lorcin has pointed out with reference to the tithe collectors of the Lyons area, if, between 1350 and 1789, 'they managed to hold their own for long periods' there was no question, as was the case for seigneurial dues, of their being able to 'drive back the enemy'.

Everyone who uses the tithe records must be aware that when one comes across written evidence of fraud in the form of accusations or trials, this indicates that the practice was well established and no doubt went back a long way; if the collector, under pressure, agrees to make any concessions, this usually indicates a definitive set-back for it would regularize a custom which until then had been considered fraudulent.

These facts, as everyone knows, should not paralyse the historian in search of tithe series, any more than errors, incomplete records or fraud have deterred historians of prices, wages or demography from collecting their basic documentation. The need for preliminary precautions and the knowledge of the difficulties involved in the use of a source must not lead to paralysis. As Labrousse reminded us at the 1977 conference, we should not exaggerate the importance of fraud 'since we are looking for trends, and hence relative results: fraud is a more or less constant factor and does not affect the *direction* of changes in income'.

Preliminary precautions

Although we should not be deterred by the question of fraud, it is true that the tithe, despite its intrinsic worth as a means of access to the 'three levels' (tithe revenue, net product, gross product) is a complex and ambiguous source, the exploitation of which necessitates some preliminary precautions.

The tithe, we must admit, is a very seductive source: it appears to be a levy raised at a fixed rate, refracting or reflecting the levels of production and characteristic, when taken over a fairly wide area, of a whole region. But we are fully aware that these attractive features conceal several traps: no serious historian has ever believed that any tithe curve could almost automatically provide us with precise and detailed information about agricultural production or yields. A tithe curve, and especially one based on a tithe paid in cash, is not a seismograph or an electrocardiogram: it is not possible to assume a direct correlation between each movement up or down and the levels of production or productivity.

The first move, rather obvious but indispensable, is to consider the amount (in kind) produced by the tithe as a function of the combination of three main factors: the rate at which the tithe was levied, the surface area of the land under consideration and the quantities produced, or the yields from this land. These three factors, alas, are far from remaining absolutely stable over time. The rate at which the tithe was levied could vary as a result of habitual resistance on the part of the peasants, or because of political changes, or even because of agreements fixed among the tithe farmers. In certain cases – to which we shall return – this level could approach or even, in exceptional times, actually reach zero: during the tithe 'strikes' of the Wars of Religion; when harvests were destroyed or collection became impossible during the Thirty Years' War; or when cereal crops failed in certain areas after the severe winter of 1708–9. It is obvious that yields varied according to the weather and also according to longer-term variations in the climate, wars, epidemics, mortality crises or the introduction of new crops. In most cases what prevents us from calculating the gross product, if not the trends which affect it, is the fact that the area subjected to the tithe may vary: 'the area under cultivation contracted during periods of war, especially civil war, or following an epidemic which had reduced the available labour supply; it expanded during peacetime or when there was an increase in population',[7] especially by means of land clearance which made the collection of the tithe difficult.

If we were trying to prove that there was always a direct correlation between the tithe and agricultural production, then – as Georges Frêche pointed out after the first survey – we would have to allow for 'the technical and legal problems affecting the tithe, and the ways in which political, military and religious developments altered its collection'.[8] However, this is not what we are trying to prove. We should point out once more that in our introduction to *Fluctuations* (Goy and Le Roy Ladurie 1972), we carefully distinguished between the two ways of analysing income derived from the tithe, general agricultural trends and the gross product, all studied over the long term. We have not changed our approach.

(1) In the last twelve years some very good series of tithe

records have been collected in France, Belgium, Hungary, Switzerland, Spain and South America: they have enabled us to formulate hypotheses which throw light on the development of the net product. There is no point at all in criticizing them for failing to provide information about trends in the gross product, in production or in yields. These records *cannot* be the basis for such an analysis of gross product. On the other hand, they do reveal upward and downward tendencies and help us to identify very long-term trends and thus have provided, and still provide us with working hypotheses which can be verified in great detail with the help of other documents.

(2) During this same period, certain exceptionally useful tithe series – mostly of tithes paid in kind, but also of some paid in money – have made it possible to produce monographs which deal with changes in the gross product in particular areas. These include the tithes of Taques d'Onnaing and Quarouble (Morineau 1970) – an exceptionally long, and hence particularly reliable, series. For this series, we know that the rate at which the tithe was levied remained constant; that, except in two or three cases of famine, there was an annual contract for the tithe paid in kind; we can check whether auctions were genuine (apart from the difficult years around 1600); we know that the overall area remained the same and in particular for the period, from 1400 to about 1590, we know the area that was in fact liable to the tithe, which makes it possible to calculate the yields per hectare, plot by plot and year by year for two centuries, and in addition to work out the theoretical minimum yields.[9]

There are also the tithe series for the area around Arles which Baehrel uncovered (Baehrel 1961) and which I have completed and integrated into a single curve. These are the vast tithes of the Chapter of Saint-Trophime in Arles, and again they were collected at a stable rate and the land area involved remained constant. The curve can be compared with a long series of yield ratios even better than Baehrel's splendid figures for two estates.[10] There are also the data collected by Hugues Neveux in his thesis on cereal crops in the Cambrésis between the end of the fourteenth century and the seventeenth (Neveux 1980, see below, pp. 40–3. Finally (without trying to be exhaustive), we should include the studies prepared for the 1977 preliminary conference by certain members of the Spanish and Hungarian research teams and by Head-Koenig and Le Goff.[11]

In all of these cases, and particularly in the most detailed monographs, each historian has taken the precaution of questioning the reliability of his source and of checking his curves against external as well as 'internal' factors. We may, *a posteriori*, reassure Georges Frêche, whose pleas for caution were made in the best critical tradition. Each historian knows whether the rates of levy in his particular area remained constant or not, and whether the tithe was collected regularly or if different crops were introduced or new land brought into cultivation; nobody has forgotten that the tithe was affected by 'the great economic, social and religious movements over the centuries – wars, the Protestant Reformation, the Catholic Counter Reformation, the insecurity of the countryside, population movements and economic trends. . . .'[12]

To be cautious is one thing; but to take refuge in overqualification and hypercriticism can 'sterilize' certain subjects by concentrating on negative conclusions.

Jean Rives' book on the tithe in the archbishopric of Auch in the eighteenth century (Rives 1976) – opportunely published by La commission d'histoire économique et sociale de la révolution française – is a delightfully thorough, coherent and erudite piece of work, but its conclusion is somewhat disappointing. Thanks to Jean Rives, we know in great detail the importance of the tithe in the archbishopric of Auch, the places and methods of collection, the tithe collectors themselves, and the effect of economic trends on the tithe (the relation between the tithe and agricultural production, tithe strikes, the crisis in the last third of the eighteenth century). He conveniently reminds us of two characteristics of the tithe which by themselves make all the precautions we have mentioned worthwhile:

(a) By definition the tithe is different from other forms of rent: 'the tithe is at the same time similar to and different from other forms of rent ... there is no doubt that the majority of men in the eighteenth century regarded it as part of the "feudal complex"; its fate was thus linked, after the night of the 4 August [abolition of feudalism by the French Constituent Assembly, 4 August 1789], with that of other feudal and seigneurial rights ... But the tithe was not a tax either ...'[13] In principle at least, it was not intended for the *seigneur* or the State, but was for 'the support of the parish clergy, the upkeep of places of worship and for works of charity'. The peculiar nature of the tithe and the fact that for a long time it had been considered a divine right no doubt explain why in the *Cahiers de Doléances* [lists of grievances submitted to the Estates], it is usually separated from the other elements of the 'feudal complex', and why it had a 'special significance', 'spiritual' as well as economic and social.

(b) Jean Rives draws attention – as we have done many times – to the main difficulties in using the tithe as a source for the eighteenth century: the lengthening of the tithe farmers' contracts, the fact that the economy was becoming more capitalist, economic decline and the increasing resistance of the peasants. He particularly stresses the fact that 'at the end of the eighteenth century, as a result of widespread refusal to pay the tithe, tithe farmers were becoming hard to find, and they tried to profit from the situation, attempting to negotiate better terms'.[14] At this period, in the area around Auch as in certain other parts of France, the tithe becomes an unreliable indicator and must either be supplemented from other sources or abandoned.

If we are disappointed by some of Jean Rives' conclusions, and by his completely negative attitude towards our attempts at quantitative analysis, this is because the objections he raises have very little to do with our interests or methods. In choosing the archbishopric of Auch, in the centre of south-west France, already 'negatively' investigated by Frêche, he has selected – as he remarks himself in justifying his study – a region where the tithe was the most significant element in the income of the clergy, the *seigneurs* and the State. Here is 'a situation which was exceptional in France', he tells us again, for 'in fact the whole economic and financial life of the region revolved around the tithe'. But the very fact that the tithe was so important meant that the rate at which it was levied, the ways it was collected, the tensions, conflicts, strikes etc. it provoked probably made it the most complex tithe – hence the most difficult to assess – in all of France! It is understandable that Rives should have chosen to disentangle the skein of tithes for the Gers region and to explain them in relation to the 'feudal complex'; it was also reasonable for him to show that resistance to the tithe was particularly strong on the eve of the French Revolution when it even led to an alliance between the lower clergy and those liable to pay the tithe; and finally, inspired by Frêche's reservations, to demonstrate that the tithe is useless as an indicator of the net and gross product in Gascony. But if his reply 'only claims to be applicable *to this region*', he ought not to draw the following conclusion at the end of the chapter on 'the tithe and agricultural production' (after stating that he had not been able – and with good reason! – to base his findings on tithe contracts alone):

Despite these reservations, the tithe can provide us with *some* information. It is true that it should be used *as an indicator of the social climate* rather than as an index of agricultural production. *However*, when used in conjunction with other data (prices, changes in population etc.) it can help to reveal the economic and social atmosphere of a region. We do not think one should *expect too much of quantitative history*, but neither should one reject it. In short, it is a useful tool for the historian, though it can be *disappointing for the economist.*[15]

What right has Rives, working on the archbishopric of Auch in the eighteenth century (an area which is obscure and inappropriate for the study of the tithe), to discredit the enormous mass of tithe data collected and analysed by Baehrel, Le Roy Ladurie, thirty or so other researchers in France and a dozen Spanish historians, not to mention some twenty colleagues from Belgium, Hungary, England, Switzerland, Quebec or Latin America?

Jean Rives informs us that it is dark in the obscurity of Gers! We take his word for it, but it would not have occurred to any historian who participated in the two collective enquiries or who has undertaken his own research into these problems to base a quantitative study of the net product, and *a fortiori* the gross product, on the tithe documents of the archbishopric of Auch – and especially not for the years from 1775 to 1789 which was the most disturbed period, but the one Rives studies at greatest length.

Let us leave the Auch tithes – with their rich potential (so well exploited) as indicators of the social and spiritual climate – in 'quantitative' peace![16]

As Le Roy Ladurie and I stated in 1972 in the final chapter of our *Fluctuations*, it would be easy to paraphrase the negative conclusions of Frêche and Rives and apply them to the major documents of the preindustrial era – parish registers, *mercurials* (market price lists), wages, goods consumed etc. – 'always distorted by objective or subjective factors. These imperfections in the documentary evidence have been known for a long time, and they have never prevented anyone from studying the history of prices or historical demography.'[17] What we have tried to do – and encouraged others to do – is 'avoid pitfalls in the old documents' by combining a 'global' view with detailed local studies. The tithe studies which have already been completed – some of which are monographs, others general studies – mark a first milestone. It cannot be denied that from the moment we reaffirmed this position we have been vindicated by the multiplication of studies of this kind, both in France and abroad. Those who had adopted a stimulating but polemical position have not prevented the exploration of this vast field, though they have caused each researcher to proceed with extreme caution and to verify his findings by checking one source against another.

One of the best examples of this type of work is that of Guy Lemeunier. In an article on 'God's share' which we have already mentioned, Lemeunier (who has done careful research on the collection of tithes in the diocese of Cartagena–Murcia in the eighteenth and nineteenth centuries) has succeeded in describing with great accuracy the mechanisms by which the tithe was collected. He drew in particular on the *Visitas de Tercias*, that is, the official records of the inspections of grain stores. He shows us 'the local authorities in their dealings with those liable to pay': for example, in the summer of 1794 a Visitor-General of the Tithes inspected eleven grain stores, thus ensuring that the diocese's third share was handled with surprising attention to detail. The employees at the granaries were questioned about their status, and about the composition of the rest of the personnel. They were also asked about the rate at which the tithe was levied, the land on which it was based and the methods of collecting it, how the tithe on cattle was assessed, the ways in which it was shared out amongst those entitled to it, and about local peculiarities in the way it was levied. They were also invited to suggest ways in which the administration of the granary could be improved.[18] It is true that Lemeunier suggests that we cannot simply assume that the level of the tithe and the extent of the land concerned remained constant. He also points out that the figures for cereal crops and cattle are more reliable than those for other agricultural products, and that the data for the nineteenth century (we are talking about Spain) are very unreliable because of the increase in fraud and in the number of exemptions. This has not prevented him, like several others working at the same time, from moving beyond the study of institutions and society and undertaking quantitative research into the development of the cereal tithe whose resulting curves, he says, 'provide us with an agricultural barometer in Murcia. They have enabled us to pinpoint the way in which tithes were farmed in this diocese, and at the same time to sketch economic trends over three centuries.'[19]

Thanks to all these precautions, Lemeunier has since been able to compile other series which help define the agricultural history of the diocese. Agricultural production is only one of the variables, and the data relating to it must be cross-checked against 'non-agricultural series, especially demographic ones, without which it is not possible to make a realistic assessment'. Such caution shows that although the historian must be critical of his sources, his criticism must not become an end in itself. Historians – positivists or pseudo-positivists – who have adopted a hypercritical approach have shown how this merely results in impotence and sterility.

A few points of method

If one is prepared to adopt a positive attitude towards tithe documents, leaving aside certain series which are very difficult or impossible to utilize, the quantitative data can be looked at in various ways, depending on whether one is dealing with tithes paid in money or in kind.

(a) Tithes paid in kind

Tithes assessed and paid in kind, whether collected directly by paid agents or farmed out to an entrepreneur, are the easiest to deal with: after compiling the series from the annual figures all one has to do is turn it into a curve on semi-logarithmic paper. This enables one to read off the short-, medium- and long-term trends and in particular to make comparisons – for example the tithe curve can be juxtaposed to price and production curves.

This is the method I adopted (together with others) to chart, for instance, the total product of the wheat tithe of the Saint-Trophime Chapter at Arles between 1660 and 1789, so as to compare this curve with the yields from seed, the acreage of land sown and the rents from the priories.[20] It does not seem necessary in these cases to use moving averages, which could give an incorrect reading and, most importantly, deny us the advantage of making an annual comparison between the tithe, the net product, and in this particular case, the gross product, reduced by fraud and various other accidents or incidents. Moving averages are not to be recommended either when one is working on wine or olive oil tithes, since in these cases the variability over two or more years is considerable and hence more statistically significant than usual. It is possible, on the other hand, to use a stepped graph for periods of ten years, which has the advantage of giving us a rapid reading of trends over one or more centuries. The final stage, when the material is available, is to draw up tithe indices for different regions. This is what I tried to do in 1968 with Head-Koenig when we drew up tithe indices for Mediterranean France from the sixteenth to the eighteenth centuries.[21] It was not a question of giving an overall picture of the tithe for the whole of the Mediterranean area of France, but of using the long series which were then available for Arles, Nice, Nîmes and Vaison-la-Romaine. These series did not by any means cover the whole area, but we felt they were representative of a zone extending from the area around Narbonne to the Maritime Alps.

The series of tithes in kind that we used were for the region around Nice, Vaison-la-Romaine, Arles, Béziers and Narbonne.

Nice: we used the grain tithe for the twelve most important areas in the hinterland of Nice. It was collected in kind

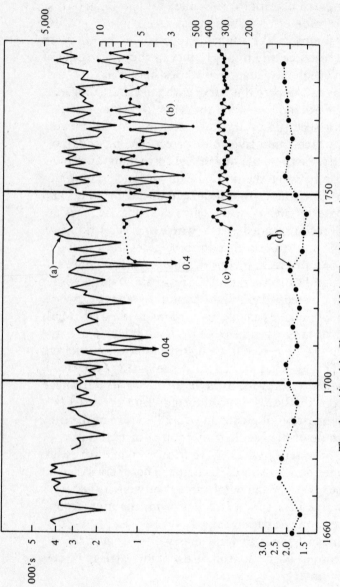

1. The wheat tithe of the Chapter of Saint-Trophime at Arles, 1660–1789

(a) = product of the wheat tithe in thousands of *setiers* for the chapter of Saint-Trophime, Arles
(b) = yield (relationship of harvest to seed) for the farms of Galignan, Couronade and Tour de Brau

(c) = quantity of seed in hundreds of *setiers* for the same 3 farms
(d) = rents of the priories of Marignane, Rognac and Velaux (each point represents the figure for a year, in hundreds of *setiers*, expressed in terms of wheat)

1 *setier* of Arles = 57.75 litres

on behalf of the Cathedral Chapter. The rate was one part in fifteen and the 'collectors' were entitled to 5% of this. The series, which is discontinuous, goes from 1698 to 1777.

Vaison-la-Romaine: the accounts of the Chapter of Vaison-la-Romaine enable us to draw up a long series from 1604 to 1776, with a few gaps, especially for the second half of the eighteenth century. The tithe in kind, known as the *bled-consegail*, was levied on the Saint-Marcellin territory at the rate of one part in eleven and a half, and wheat accounted for 80% of the total.

Arles: the data for Arles cover most of the land around the town, in other words, the four main areas (Trébon, Plan-du-Bourg, Crau and Camargue) plus the territory of Fourgues. We used the 'great' wheat tithe (froment, touzelle blanche ou rouge et saissette, beau bled, soulens et soulensons). The fine series for Plan-du-Bourg spans the period 1558 to 1788, while the other areas provide us with continuous data from 1662 to 1788.

Béziers: the 'great' wheat tithe of Béziers, paid in kind, was normally farmed out, but occasionally the Chapter was itself responsible for collecting it. The results are scarcely different, since the farmer's profit was essentially in straw, or possibly in secondary cereals such as barley or oats. The series goes from 1550 to 1764 with a few gaps.

Narbonne: the cereal tithe, levied by the Chapter of Saint-Just and Saint-Pasteur of Narbonne, was collected from seven localities (Cuxac, La Plaine et Livière, Salies, Ouveillan, Moussan, Creisson and Celairan). These series cover the period 1532 to 1776.

Unfortunately these series were discontinuous, beginning and ending at different dates, so before we could use them to produce an overall picture of the whole region, we had to work out a method of indexing. This was done in four stages. First, we chose the decade 1765–74 as representing the base of 100. This was a period for which we had the greatest number of continuous series, and which was neither too prosperous nor too depressed, with a reasonable spread of good and bad harvests. The tithes in kind from the various areas were then calculated in relation to this base, two adjustments being necessary in the case of Saint-Nazaire at Béziers and of Saint-Just at Narbonne, where there were no data for the period 1765–74.

Imagine a series A, which has gaps in it. The readjustment consists in establishing for the year before the lacuna the index of all the other series, and proceeding from there. Suppose series A has a gap from 1749 to 1788, while B, C and D provide data from 1750 onwards. The average figure for 1749 is calculated for series B, C and D. This average is applied to series A for 1749 which allows series A to be 'indexed' for the years before 1749 (using the period 1765–74 as a base).

In taking the average of all these indices without weighting, we obtained an index for tithes in kind, which we then used as a basis for comparison with other indices of tithe revenues in money. This method has also been used by Bernard Garnier for the Lieuvin area of Normandy between the beginning of the seventeenth century and 1779.[22] But it was Hugues Neveux who developed this method in the most rigorous and convincing way; he explains it at length in his thesis on cereals in the Cambrésis.[23]

In order to study the rise and fall of agricultural production in the Cambrésis, he attempted to isolate the 'grain' component by using the abundant and relatively homogeneous records of the Notre-Dame Chapter at Caen, the Collegiate Church of Saint-Géry, the abbey of Saint-Sepulchre and the Saint-Julien Hospital. There were enough series to make 'quantitative' analysis possible, but not so many that they could not be exhaustively exploited. This necessitated a 'survey based on samples, an alternative which affects the methods employed and necessitates certain choices from the start'. This kind of work based on samples offers several advantages:

Methodology

(1) It is possible to 'concentrate on a few homogeneous series' and 'to construct the indices one requires only from the most reliable and the most suitable series'.

(2) It considerably reduces 'the risk of error implicit in the manipulation of any unprocessed data'. The success of this type of research depends, however, on the choice of sources used as samples. The areas to be considered, for example, should be 'fairly large units, distributed over a wide geographical area' and they should be cases where 'the ecclesiastical nature of the records does not distort the figures'.

The sources used by Hugues Neveux are *dîmeries*, that is, 'a collection of different levies on the harvests', in other words, actual managerial units of the share of the gross agricultural product taken by the Church. It is necessary to select *dîmeries* for their size and also their distribution. Passing from the *dîmerie* to the sample, and from the sample to the whole zone, it becomes possible to study both 'global' and regional development. To do this one must concentrate not just on extending the series (since this merely creates further objects for study), nor on analysing each series in detail (which only tells us more about that particular case), but on confronting one process with the other. Since these series of dues (and of course the same thing applies to prices) constitute indirect indices of production in the long, medium and even short term, 'the confrontation of evidence from different types of series narrows the field of possibility and reinforces the probability of one set of these indirect indices'. It ensures the elimination of purely local factors and defines the extent and value of the indices.[24] The third task is to collect the qualitative data which are absolutely essential for an understanding of the series and the curves, and which may, in certain cases, fill some of the gaps in the quantitative data. Thus the preparation of samples, the construction of series and the process of examining them side by side, together with the collection of complementary, explanatory quali-

41

tative data allow us to study three things: the variations in cereal production, the main factors affecting the interpretation of these fluctuations and, hence, the 'rise and fall of an economic structure'.

The preliminary work – which involves taking a broad sample of tithes representing a considerable volume – is important in 'eliminating the influence of local conditions ... evening out the variations in the amounts raised from different fields (or at different rates, or because there were several parties entitled to share the dues), and providing a body of data which is sufficiently sensitive to slight oscillations in production'.

Confronting one set of data with others then reduces the risk of error to a minimum. Let us say that a given series shows a very marked positive or negative tendency: if the other series in the same collection do not show the same characteristics this means that the 'atypical' series is reflecting local conditions (rates of levy, discrepancies in assessment, or a local strike). But if all the series are similarly affected, one may reasonably conclude that the tendency in question is not merely the result of isolated circumstances but reflects a change in production trends at a regional or more general level.

For the Cambrésis, in the two centuries studied, 'in the long term the trend in the tithe essentially reflects the fluctuations in the gross product'. As a result of all these precautions, it is possible to detect the influence of purely local factors, to reduce changes in measurement and in market dues to their rightful proportions, and to take into account differences in the tithe farmer's profit, which was on the average 15%, but could vary from 10 to 20%. For the study of short-term trends Hugues Neveux suggests replacing the tithe index (which for the Cambrésis is not suitable for this type of analysis) by an index derived from the annual payments made by the tithe farmer, depending on the level of production. Although this is not an ideal solution, it can yield useful data for short-term periods.[25]

Methodology

We cannot deal here with all the possible uses of Hugues Neveux's proposed method. By studying the data for tithes in kind and the sums paid by the tithe farmers, as well as price and population figures, he has been able to go well beyond the study of 'cereals' mentioned in the title of his thesis. From now on researchers have access not only to the numerous monographs (listed above) which have appeared in the last twenty years, but also to a very substantial piece of work devoted almost entirely to the tithe paid in kind, its value, the ways in which it can be used and its relation to overall agricultural production.

(b) Tithes paid in money

It is clear that tithes paid in money, which constitute the largest body of records, cannot be used the same way in attempts to discern the development of the net product, and ideally, the main trends in the gross product. These series of tithes paid in money and the curves which they have produced can already tell us a great deal. They give an indication of the tithe income in the currency of the period, and can begin to yield interesting data if one takes the trouble to compare them with price curves, beginning with wheat. But it is not enough to plot the curves for a tithe paid in money and for wheat prices on the same graph: not everyone is capable of 'correcting' the tithe curve with the help of the price curve. A more satisfying method is to 'deflate' the cash tithe by expressing it in terms of its equivalent in kind. This can be done by dividing the money tithe by a price index. According to Paul Samuelson's definition, deflation means expressing a sum of money in terms of real goods, and in the case of the tithe, this means dividing the sum received annually by the current price of the chosen foodstuff (usually wheat).[26] One could say that changes in the amount of rent of the tithe farms (between 10–15%) approximate changes in the revenue from tithes paid in money, in other words, to use Le Roy Ladurie's phrase, 'the least inaccurate approximation which the statistical *ancien régime* affords on trends in the potential revenue of a given piece of land, at the prices of the time'.[27] At first sight, this movement appears nothing more than 'the general trend of the harvest, reflecting the prices for each individual crop'. In this case and for every tithe based on all the products of a piece of land but paid annually in cash, one should use a composite index derived from the prices of wheat, barley, oats, rye, wine, oil, sheep etc. – in other words, a price index calculated according to the proportions of each product of which the tithe was composed. This, of course, is an impossible undertaking: it presupposes a knowledge of crop proportions for a given tithe, whereas in fact the documents – which refer to a tithe 'translated' into cash – do not tell us so much. We must therefore give up the attempt to work out a deflating index of this kind – it is an attractive idea but simply not practicable. This invites us to adopt a simpler system, which is by no means perfect but which at least has the merit of enabling us to make comparisons among the available tithe series. As we have already explained, these tithes, paid in cash, were farmed out, which means that lessees contracted (either by negotiating directly with the lessor, or as a result of auctions) to pay the lessor a certain sum for a period of three, five, six or very occasionally nine years. The sum agreed was a compromise between two conflicting assessments of the situation: that of the lessor, who was well aware of previous returns, his expenses and the need to increase his profit; and that of the lessee which is rather more complicated since he had to take into account five factors at once:

(a) the risk of losing the deal to a rival if he offered too little;

(b) his estimate of the harvest, based on those of previous years. To reduce the risk he would calculate what he could expect in an average year;

(c) the sum he could hope to get by reselling the tithe paid to him in kind – in other words, an estimate of future market conditions;

(d) the expense he would incur in collecting the tithe, i.e. the wages he would have to pay his men, plus transport and storage costs;

(e) the level of profit he wanted (usually between 10 and 15%).

This is enough to show that, at least from the seventeenth century onwards and no doubt on earlier occasions, this system of organizing the tithe collection, and the large sums of money involved, represented a form of rural capitalism. The tithe farmers could, in certain cases, be seen as genuine capitalist entrepreneurs who transformed a due, paid in kind and subject to harvest fluctuations, into a cash income. The largest part would go to the owners of the tithe and another part, distinctly smaller, would be retained to cover the expenses of collection and to produce a profit. By agreeing to farm the tithes they were undeniably taking a risk because of the unstable nature of production, unforeseeable variations in the market and external factors such as strikes, wars or epidemics.

Having taken all this into account, it is nonetheless desirable to deflate these series of 'cash tithes' by using a price index which in most cases should be based on grain prices, since these are a major element in production and consumption. It is also desirable to 'temper' this deflation by using a moving average of prices calculated from several sets of figures (from seven to thirteen) when the contracts themselves cover several years. It would be misleading to use annual prices to deflate series spanning three, six or nine years. One of the difficulties of this kind of deflation is that continuous series of grain prices are rare; all we can do under these conditions is to use a price series derived from an area located as close as possible to the area being studied.

Let us look at a few examples of this method of calculating the tithe in terms of grain equivalent.

When Head-Koenig and I were compiling our Mediterranean tithe index we tried, for the first time for such a large region, to use all the available series of tithes paid in money.[28] (In his *Paysans de Languedoc*, Le Roy Ladurie had already worked out the wheat equivalent for the tithe from the Cathedral Chapter of Montpellier.)[29]

We were able to draw on the tithes or the rents of tithe farms paid in money to the Chapters of Montpellier, Béziers, Narbonne, Arles, Aix and Nîmes. It is clear that in this case we were not concerned with cereal crops alone, but with all the products on which the tithe was levied.

Montpellier: we looked at the revenue from the priories of the Chapter of Saint-Pierre, which derived almost entirely from the tithe. The series extends from 1567 to 1789, with a few gaps.

Béziers: the index was compiled from the 'ordinary revenue' or the 'priory revenue', again derived essentially from the tithe. This income came entirely from the countryside, from twenty parishes or priories. The data used cover the period 1558–1769, but there are many gaps.

Narbonne: the accounts for the Saint-Just Chapter at Narbonne do not provide us with the total tithe income. So in order to obtain an average for the period 1530–1777, we had to construct an index for each of the twenty-seven priories based on tithe contracts.

Arles, Aix and Marseilles: the priories of Marignane, Rognac and Velaux (depending on Saint-Trophime at Arles), Salernes (depending on Saint-Victor at Marseilles), Eguilles and Meyreuil (Saint-Sauveur at Aix) provided us with leases for each five-year period from 1600 to 1785. The figures involved correspond, for the most part, to the grain tithe.

Nîmes: the records at Nîmes provide us with tithe figures for thirty-nine priories attached to the Saint-Castor Chapter. These priories varied in size and income, and also in the relative importance of the various tithes. Only eleven of these thirty-nine priories provided us with data for the sixteenth century. The series goes from 1555 to 1786.

Methodology

The data concerning tithes paid in cash are much more varied, so that we were obliged to use a more complicated method here than for the index of tithes paid in kind.

The total tithe income for Saint-Pierre at Montpellier and Saint-Nazaire at Béziers were analysed statistically in exactly the same way as the tithes in kind.

Since the Saint-Just Chapter at Narbonne did not provide us with the total annual income from the tithe, we had to draw up a table of tithe contracts based on five-year periods for each of the twenty-seven priories, and then calculate an average index for this. The same method was applied for the priories of Marignane, Rognac, Velaux, Salernes, Meyreuil and Eguilles.

For the Nîmes data, we distinguished two groups of priories, twenty-three in one and sixteen in the other, which furnished two partial indices from which we calculated an average.

The five indices thus obtained gave us an average overall index of tithes paid in cash. This was expressed in terms of wheat by means of a moving average of wheat prices in Toulouse (see Figure 2). Although Toulouse was relatively far away, we used the series of wheat prices compiled by Geneviève and Georges Frêche.[30] The prices available for Aix and for the market at Béziers do not cover the three centuries studied.

The final stage, which should not be seen as the main aim of our research, was to calculate an index of the income derived from the tithe, either in kind or in money, for the Mediterranean area of France. This index is unfortunately composite and we are well aware of its shortcomings. To obtain it, the money index (expressed in terms of the equivalent value of wheat) had to be integrated with the tithe-in-kind index: it was therefore multiplied by the value of the relation between the 'money index' and the 'kind index' for the decade 1765–74. The average of these two indices was then used to work out the Mediterranean index.

To emphasize the experimental nature of our method we

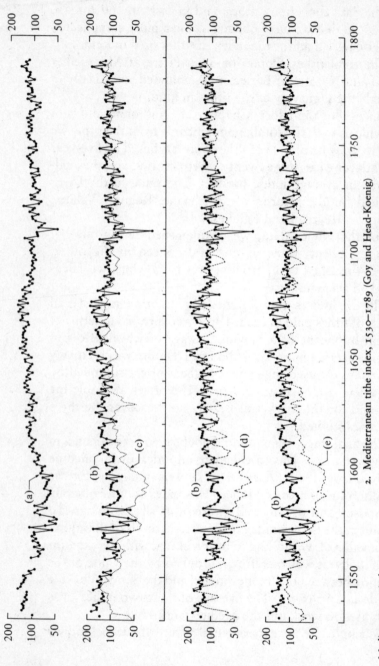

2. Mediterranean tithe index, 1530–1789 (Goy and Head-Koenig)

(a) = Mediterranean index
(b) = index of tithes paid in kind
(c) = index of tithe revenues in money deflated by 7-year moving
      average, calculated every 4th year

(d) = index of tithe revenues in money deflated by 3-year moving
      average, calculated every 4th year
(e) = index of tithe revenues in money deflated by 7-year moving
      average, calculated every 8th year

1765–74 = 100

have since carried out various statistical tests on the number of terms making up the moving average. The overall average index of the tithe paid in money has been deflated successively by moving averages based on the figures for three and seven years, and calculated in the fourth and eighth years respectively. Take, for example, the year 1750 in the series of money tithes: if one uses a three-year moving average, one can deflate it by taking the moving average for wheat prices in 1747, 1748 and 1749; and if one is using a seven-year moving average, the same thing is done for 1743, 1744, 1745, 1746, 1747, 1748 and 1749. It goes without saying that to make comparisons easier the overall money-indices thus obtained are then integrated with the overall tithe-in-kind index. It must also be said that attempts to express the index in terms of grammes of pure silver or in terms of food consumption – in other words in terms of the 'shopping basket' containing bread, wine, meat, oil – have not led to any useful results.

On the other hand, we have made no attempt to assess the relative importance of the various pieces of land on which the tithe was levied, nor of the various priories attached to a Chapter, nor of the overall data for tithes in money in relation to those concerning tithes paid in kind. In other words, all the units of land on which the tithe was levied – no matter how large they were or how much they produced – were weighted equally in the calculation of our index. Having made these reservations, we should remind the reader that the aim of this experiment was to analyse the existing tithe sources using a method which we knew was open to improvement. It made possible the study of tithe trends over a considerable area for two and a half centuries, and confirmed, we believe, certain evidence concerning the long-term movement of the tithe and of the net product. These curves (see Figure 2) do reveal the movement, over quite a long period, of two related variables: ecclesiastical income and the overall trend in agriculture (taking into account production, the options open to tithe farmers, and attempts to predict demand).

The same methods were adopted for a smaller area by Bernard Garnier in his study of the Chapters of Coutances, Lisieux and Bayeux (Garnier 1975). He used the series of Paris prices and the *apprécies* of Coutances and transformed them into indices to make comparisons easier: his article shows a remarkable co-variance between the tithes paid in kind and those paid in money when the latter are expressed in real terms. When applied carefully to suitable material these results show that this method can yield excellent results.

Normandy has been the subject of a number of other tithe studies. For an earlier period, from the fourteenth to the middle of the sixteenth centuries, in his thesis on the rural economy and demography of eastern Normandy (Bois 1976), Guy Bois attempts to establish various economic indices, and especially, that of the important gross product.[31] To do this, Bois could draw on 'only one source, and an imprecise one at that: the revenue from the tithes'. He was aware that the tithe curves could only produce 'an approximate picture of production',[32] but he nevertheless felt the attempt was worth making. Bois had to preface his work with a critique of his disparate and discontinuous data – he was not dealing with the seventeenth or eighteenth centuries, but beginning in 1377 and ending in 1527. He raised the question of the validity of the tithe as a source for economic history and discussed the problems encountered in interpreting it. He noted for his region – as other researchers have done for theirs –

that the contracts for one year showed a closer correlation between the rent paid by the tithe farmer and the actual value of the harvest than the three-year contracts of the sixteenth century did. In the latter case the farmer took a higher risk and so expected a greater share;

that the 'overwhelming preponderance of cereals' in agricultural production meant that 'trends in cereal production were certainly representative of production as a whole';

that if the series are not sufficiently continuous it is not possible to deflate them;

and that from the first third of the sixteenth century, as during the period 1436–50, the data are seriously affected by a general climate of tithe evasion.

In spite of these reservations, and a few others relating to the extreme sensitivity of urban prices, Guy Bois has calculated the average receipts from the different tithe farms, and the average price of a measure of wheat and a measure of oats added together ('deflated', i.e. the period 1399–1405 has been taken as a base (= 100) and the main trend calculated, the short-term fluctuations being eliminated). He recognizes, as we did, the limitations of his method; Guy Bois suggests that the margin of error is around 20–25%, which rules out any precise interpretation of the results, but does allow a few general observations on the agricultural product.

These three examples (and there are many others amongst the studies presented at the two conferences of 1969 and 1977 relating to completely different areas and periods) reveal the difficulties which are universally encountered when dealing with the data for tithes paid in money, but they also indicate the hypotheses and sometimes even certainties which emerge when the series are treated carefully and systematically.

Every researcher working on a series of tithes paid in money has noticed the three effects pointed out by A. Eiras Roel at the 1977 conference:[33]

(a) a 'concealing' or masking effect when the length of certain contracts means that certain poor harvests can pass unnoticed;

(b) a 'flattening' effect of the deflating process, when the use of a moving average spreads over several years the impact of a sharp price increase which took place in one year;

(c) a 'displacing' effect when, again, the use of a moving average means that a distorting index may be applied to certain years.

The problems resulting from the incidence of these effects are of little significance when compared with the value of the mass of results obtained from the tithe data listed in the Appendix to Chapter 1. This is all the more true in that advances are constantly being made in the use of the tithe as a source: Hugues Neveux, for example, devised a more rigorous method in his work on the Cambrésis (Neveux 1980). Hungarian scholars have used a greater mass of data from exceptionally long series, and the use of the computer has meant that it has made it possible to work out per capita productivity for certain Hungarian series. In the case of the tithes studied for the Berne area, Charles Pfister has developed a more refined statistical method (the cluster analysis) to overcome the problems posed by the mass of data involved (100,000 items) and the fact that he was dealing with nineteen different local measures and five types of grain. By grouping within curves the same area, and then areas in the regions, and by converting all measures into hectolitres and kilograms, Pfister has succeeded in elaborating a model capable of providing us with the rate at which the tithe was levied, the area under cultivation, the yields from seed and the farmer's profit, together with the effects of all these factors on the price of the tithe farms. This method enabled him to pick out zones where correlations were strong, and to formulate hypotheses about the rôle of certain variables within the general trends.

This progress in the selection of samples and in methods of analysis has had some secondary effects: not only can tithe curves be used to show trends and indicate the different periodicity of different variables, but they also reflect a number of natural, economic and social phenomena. As Michel Morineau hoped, in his 'afterthoughts and a look ahead',[34] each historian working on the tithe is increasingly concerned with 'seeing each curve as an entity, the product of several variables', with isolating and analysing these variables, and with assembling these curves in families and interpreting them 'without trying to fit them into any preconceived theoretical structure'. It should not be forgotten that the same historians involved in developing these techniques often use other methods for studying the history of the agricultural product. There can be useful interaction between the various approaches.

Other methods

There are obvious cases, such as Poland and Italy, where it is not possible to use the tithe as a source. There are others for which the tithe data, even in series, do not have the same significance as in the economies of most Western European or Latin American countries. In Quebec, for example, as Paquet and Wallot have shown,[35] the tithe and ground rents 'do not constitute adequate indicators for estimating agricultural trends or measuring production and peasant income in preindustrial Quebec. They cannot, *a fortiori*, reflect any overall trend.' It is not because these sources are hard to find but because of 'the original features of economic reality in Canada around 1840', since in Quebec, for example, the economy revolved around the timber trade rather than agriculture. As Wallot pointed out at the 1977 conference, 'when people reached subsistence level, they were happy to remain there and to seek any supplementary income they needed elsewhere, in particular by woodcutting'. The Quebec tithes, which were paid in kind and at a very low rate (in the seventeenth century) did not provoke any serious opposition and at least show us to what extent the parishes were under cultivation.

The tithes for such 'peripheral' regions with colonial-style economies cannot, then, be satisfactory indicators of the economic and social development of these new and rapidly expanding countries where trade is always much more important than agriculture. In such cases, the 'forces or drives of population and production' are not necessarily linked, for it is a question of a small population settling on fertile land and working its way into trade circuits which themselves feed into the international markets.

In many other cases where it is again impossible to use the tithe – in the Paris region for instance,[36] where the tithe was simply levied at a fixed rate per acre and did not represent a percentage of the harvest – one can use the estate leases: these documents can also render long series and give us an idea of the development of the estate revenues, in other words, of ground rents. During the 1966 tithe enquiry the work done on ground rents was fairly limited. There were the studies already mentioned of Le Roy Ladurie and Veyrassat-Herren, and of Desaive, dealing respectively with the Paris region, the ground rents around Lyons and the Knights of Saint John.[37] The second collection of studies in 1977 was much richer in this respect, since most of the contributors tried wherever possible to make parallel studies of the tithe movement and that of ground rents.[38] Neither is it an accident that the most comprehensive of these studies have been produced by French and Belgian historians: Béaur's work on ground rents around Chartres in the eighteenth century, Butel on wine production and ground rents in the Bordelais in the eighteenth century, Chéreau and Michel on leases in the Anjou and Le Mans regions (seventeenth and eighteenth centuries), Constant on the Beauce (from the sixteenth to the eighteenth century) and Garnier and Pavard on ground rents in Normandy, Maine and Anjou. There are also the studies put together by Van der Wee for the Edinburgh conference (*Proceedings* 1). It was this collection that Van der Wee and Van Cauwenberghe drew on in 1977 when they sent us their valuable paper on productivity, trends in tithe rents and the size of farms in the Netherlands from the fourteenth to the eighteenth centuries.[39] The series of tithe contracts used provide extremely precise information, over the very long term, about the type and distribution of the plots of land involved, their surface area, the duration of the leases, the number of years specified, the social position of the tithe farmer, the dates on which the agreed sum fell due, and the nature and amount of the 'farm' to be paid. The discussion about the place, rôle and ways of measuring ground rents is indeed central to rural history and even more to quantitative history, after the work of Simiand, Labrousse, Meuvret, Goubert and many others. But it is Jean Jacquart who has stated the issues most clearly. In his thesis on the rural crisis in the Ile-de-France, 1550–1670 (Jacquart 1974), as well as in his pioneer study of 1975 on ground rents, as an index of trends,[40] he stressed the particular importance of understanding this category of income, which had previously been used rather less than prices and products for studying economic trends. As far as sources are concerned, ground rents appear to present some of the same problems as the tithe. One can find oneself faced with *baux à part de fruit* (share-cropping), a form widespread in the agricultural economy of the *ancien régime* but which makes calculating the rent difficult. There are also, of course, composite leases where there is no differentiation between the revenue from the 'farm', the 'feudal' dues and other sources of income. Documents concerning farming out of plots of land are affected by other sorts of problems, again derived from their composite nature. In short, this type of lease demands the greatest critical attention both in drawing up series for estates or plots of land, and in choosing an index to deflate them, since it could prove too sensitive (for example wheat prices) or liable to conceal certain economic and social effects. Even if 'the best series of contracts, like the best tithe series, can tell us no more than what it contains', there have been enough studies in the last few years to enable us to outline the trends in ground rents from the sixteenth century to the Revolution.[41] But in addition to this outline, with its 're-assuring agreement of evidence', Jacquart invites us to think about the significance of rent. It is even more ambiguous than the tithe. If it 'represents a share in what is left of the farm product once the latter's basic survival is assured . . . it is still only one of the elements involved – the gross product is also shared between the tithe, seigneurial dues, state taxes and the agriculturalist's profit'. It is clear, then, that rents are linked to production and the market value of the land, and have an *economic* relation to the quantities produced and the prices obtained. But since the rent is agreed upon by contract, it is also affected by the relative strength of the negotiating parties. So it is not 'a straightforward economic relation': it is true that the rent is an additional indicator which is extremely useful for studying the fluctuations of the net product and sometimes of the gross product, especially when used in conjunction with indicators based on the tithe and on prices. But still more obviously, it also reveals the social tensions between those who owned the land and those who worked it, and in this way it can be seen as a good *social* index. The most recent studies of Normandy – those by Hugues Neveux and Bernard Garnier on the value of the land, agricultural production and urban markets in the seventeenth century; by Bernard Garnier on the structure and trends of rents in Upper Maine in the seventeenth and eighteenth centuries and by Gabriel Desert on the landowners and estates of the Norman Bocage in the nineteenth century – show that rural history is now much concerned with rents as well as with prices and production.[42] The same could be said about the research done in Eastern Europe on the shift from rents paid in money to rents paid in labour.[43]

Much work has been done recently on grain yields as well as on the tithe and on ground rents. Following the pioneer work of Slicher Van Bath and J. Z. Titow,[44] studies of the productivity of the land have made considerable progress but they have not enabled us, except in a few cases, to compile very long series for representative areas in France (this is not true for England or Prussia). Besides, since most studies refer to one plot of land, or at most to one farm, it is very difficult to use the curves obtained as an index of the long-term trends in cereal production. At best, they can be used to verify certain curves relating to production. Studies like those of Michel Morineau for France (Morineau 1970), Maurice Aymard for Sicily,[45] Head-Koenig for Germany and Switzerland,[46] Ponsot for Spain,[47] or my own on four farms near Arles (which completes the data for the two studied by Baehrel)[48] are too isolated and scattered over too wide an area to give us an overall picture, even if they have supplied useful data about the productivity of the land.

The only systematic enquiry was undertaken by Hugues Neveux under the auspices of the Centre de Recherches d'Histoire Quantitative at Caen, directed by Pierre Chaunu.[49] It began in 1975 with the study of above- and below-average harvests from the fourteenth to the nineteenth centuries. It drew widely on the data collected by Titow and of the important contribution of Marie-Jeanne Tits-Dieuaide (on cereal prices in Brabant and Flanders).[50] Via an index of yield ratios, the aim was to establish the relation between the size of the harvest and the level of prices. Mme Tits-Dieuaide later joined a group which, while retaining this method of analysing yields, attempted to study them not as one of the factors determining prices but for their own sake. It was organized as a comparative study at the regional, national and international level.

The first stage of the project resulted in a structural study of the short-term fluctuations in cereal yields in north-western Europe from the fourteenth to the sixteenth century published by Neveux and Tits-Dieuaide.[51] Instead of considering sudden changes in the rate of production from the point of view of their causes, effects and position in socio-economic structures and processes, the Caen team collected numerous series of yields from seed. These related to the south of England and the regions around Louvain and Brussels, and they 'were well distributed in time and space'.[52] For all these series, using a programme of information processing, they measured the fluctuations in yields (dispersion) and the co-variance of the yields of the main cereal crops for a given period. A similar method was used by Van der Wee and Van Cauwenberghe in their preliminary studies for the Paris and Edinburgh conferences.[53]

The project showed, as we shall see later, that the variability of yields was a much more complex problem than had been realized, and it helped to shape a new type of research, which would try 'to establish a geography and chronology of fluctuations in yields on a European scale until the time when these fluctuations levelled off'.

Altogether, a dozen years of individual and collective research have undeniably increased our knowledge of the development of the tithe, the net product, the gross product and hence of production and productivity. As Labrousse reminded us at Compostela, none of these phenomena, apart from the tithe, is as well known as price trends; whereas the price of the main products was a 'public fact', the farmers were not in the habit of declaring their harvest figures unless they were forced to do so. The curves which have been produced are not as homogeneous as those for prices: they reveal distortions and anomalies at a' local, regional or national level, which enables us to see the trends provided we interpret them in terms of maxima and minima and admit that there is a considerable margin of uncertainty. This uncertainty is due to the fact that we have deliberately chosen to study long-term trends over several centuries (although we still need to extend the time span by involving specialists in medieval and ancient history). We must bear in mind that the factors we are concerned with may not remain constant over this very long period. We cannot be totally confident, either, in the indices obtained by means of deflation, or in other words, by expressing a sum of money in terms of its grain equivalent. Here, the use of moving averages may distort the impact of certain phenomena over the medium term and displace, or even wipe out their effect over the short term. Despite its lack of precision, this simple method has given some good results, especially when the series of prices used have been closely related. This makes it much easier to distinguish the long-term phenomena and to identify trends, which can then be checked against other sources.

It is also unfortunate that, so far, our research has been largely restricted to cereal production, since this was over-whelmingly important in the old agricultural economy. From now on, if the sources permit, we should concentrate on investigating the development of other crops, regional variations, and the often under-estimated rôle of stock-breeding and shrub-crops – in short, on the changes in the structure of production. On the whole, we have reached a better understanding of agricultural societies. One thing is clear: there were differences between these societies at the regional, national and international levels. There were con-trasts between the centre and the periphery of each geo-graphical area, as the Spanish historians have indicated, and there were also distinctions between the three zones identified by Le Roy Ladurie at the 1977 conference:

(a) the Atlantic, Mediterranean and Catholic areas of Europe, where the tithe registers reflect, more or less accu-rately, levies on all the products of the land, cereals in par-ticular, and where the tithe contracts reveal the relations and tensions between the owners and the tithe farmers;

(b) the north, east and continental areas of Europe, dominated by the nobility and the state. Here, the tithes were often secularized, converted into dues and levied arbi-trarily so that they are not a very reliable means of measur-ing production. To construct reliable indices the historian must use the records from the great estates, taking into account (especially when measuring productivity) the im-portant, but not always easily assessed, rôle of the *corvée*;

(c) the peripheral, colonial agricultural systems, charac-terized either by an agricultural sector which was insignifi-cant compared with lumbering and trade (Quebec), or by very marked inequalities between settlers and natives, masters and slaves, which emerged as a result of the development of the mining sector and of speculative crops such as sugar or coffee (Latin America); in both cases the agricultural system was 'mobile', in other words, there was a migrant agricultural population which shifted as new land came into cultivation.

After the initial work on establishing the major trends has been completed, we now have the possibility of exploiting in a new way, not only the sources already mentioned, but also other similar ones.

nʊmʊmʊmʊmʊmʊmʊmʊmʊmʊmʊmʊmʊmʊmʊmʊmʊmʊmʊmʊmʊmʊm ʊmʊmʊmʊmʊmʊmʊmʊmʊm

Towards another kind of history of the tithe, production and productivity

It is obvious that, in this rapid description of sources and methods, it has not been possible to mention all the studies of rural societies concerned with dues, production and productivity. The tithe, ground rents and estate accounts are not the only documents which can be used, and there are many trails still to be explored. Let us give two examples. French historians have perhaps not paid enough attention to sources which, while not really serial, are often very precise and entirely suitable for the study of the gross product over the short and medium term. These include, for example, the declarations of income made by the priests of France in the eighteenth century: in 1701 the general assembly of French clergy, which was responsible for deciding how much each diocese had to contribute towards the king's *don gratuit*, organized a national survey. On at least three occasions in the eighteenth century (in 1728, 1751 and 1760) the priests returned information on their income and these documents, preserved partly in the Archives Nationales, in G8, and partly in the departmental archives, enable us to make cross-sections and to form some impression of the gross product.[1]

The records of the *champart* constitute another source very similar to the tithe, at least when the *champart* takes its original form as a percentage of the harvest paid to the landowner or his agent: this type of source, which can even include details of the size of the land or plot involved and the quantity of grain harvested, presupposes a working knowledge of the rate at which this due was levied, of the weight of grain per sheaf (a favourite topic for specialists in production), of the amount of seed used, and of the old agricultural units of measurement. One can then obtain relatively reliable data about production and the productivity of the land.

However, even if other documents so far unexploited allowed us to refine our knowledge of certain sectors and short periods, none of them can cover the same wide area, in time and space, as tithe records, leases or farm accounts. We can see how this wealth of documentation has led to attempts to find new ways of exploiting it: such sources have undeniably resulted in a renewed interest in the history of agricultural production, and it is no doubt possible and desirable that they should also be used to solve other problems relating to agricultural history.

Let us note first that some recent research, presented at the Edinburgh conference, is not only concerned with trends in prices, production, and productivity: the same indicator can, in fact, reflect various realities in different systems of production. For example, in the case of the great estates of the Roman Campagna in the seventeenth and eighteenth centuries (studied by Jacques Revel), the data on yields turn out to be very relative economic indicators.[2] It is an area which experienced a 'premature blockage in agricultural production, or at least, an increasing inertia in production in the face of the demands from the urban market'. This, according to Revel, was due to the restrictions on prices and profits imposed by the Roman administration (*annona*), and – and this is Revel's particular contribution – to the way in which the great estate was organized: it was 'ill-adapted in that it only yielded limited productivity in return for a considerable investment'. The study of wheat yields enabled Revel to note several incompatible, but significant, features:

(1) long-term stability fails to hide a downward trend in the second half of the eighteenth century – a decline which reflects both the exhaustion of poor soils and the attempt

to compensate for this by increasing the amount of seed used per square metre;

(2) the fairly low level of yields for Italy points towards a triple 'lethargy' in production, ground rents and the farmer's profit due not only to the 'blockage' of prices, but also to the fact that returns on investment, which was a significant element in this region, were not as high as they should have been because investment was concerned only with the upkeep of the estate and not with technical improvements. In this case, we are dealing with a form of agriculture in which there was a high level of investment, but which, like the traditional smallholding, relied on good harvests to make a little profit. If calculations of the yields are to be fully significant, they must be assessed in relation to the amount of capital invested as well as in relation to the surface area or the amount of labour involved;

(3) in the case of a family smallholding, the yield clearly does not have the same significance and these factors do not apply.

It is enough to point out that if one is using a single indicator for different regions and different systems of production, one must be careful to replace it in the overall socio-economic context.

A. Poitrineau was aware of these issues in his research on animal and vegetable production in the mountains of the Auvergne in the eighteenth century.[3] He studied the pattern of trade between the mountains and the outside world: the inhabitants of the mountains had to buy vegetable products, especially cereals, because they could not produce enough for their needs; the only way they could do this was to produce a surplus of livestock for the market. This trading pattern was affected by the normal fluctuations in prices, by increasing demographic pressure, and by the lack of flexibility in animal production (it was very difficult to increase animal production for technical reasons and because of restrictions on space – it was not possible to reduce cereal production). This pattern could lead, as was the case in the eighteenth century, to a rapid process of impoverishment of these mountain people as the price of vegetable products increased at a faster rate than that of animal products. This led Poitrineau to suggest undertaking a general study of 'the mountain areas which had gone in for stockbreeding, of the crucial differences in the prices of imported and exported animal and vegetable products, of the resulting socio-demographic tensions and of the shifts in population' provoked by the process of impoverishment set in motion by all these factors.

Jean Nicolas' work on Savoy in the eighteenth century has led him to adopt a very critical attitude towards tithe documents, but he also recommends another way of exploiting them: to regard them not just as an indicator of the gross product, but also, and perhaps more importantly, as a social indicator, since the tithe is a due levied on peasant income.[4]

Nicolas recognizes that the tithe has offered – and will continue to offer – important information about certain types of trend, as shown in the studies carried out in the last ten years. But his work on Savoy leads him to suggest that the tithe should be considered from two angles:

(1) the first approach is common to all who use the tithe as a source: it involves examining the tithe records at 'surface level' in order to establish the nature and the evolution of the harvests, the changes over time, and how this income compares with other types of income. The series and curves obtained for Savoy in the eighteenth century[5] show that the 'good years 1660–90' were followed by a period of deteriorating harvests in 1690–1700, caused by 'poor weather and military activity', and this was in turn followed by a period of real decline. This 'decline', however, was only relative as far as agriculture was concerned: what was declining was the tithe itself as an institution. It was becoming less significant because of resistance on the part of the peasants – resistance which sometimes went as far as revolt but more commonly expressed itself in

obstructive measures, by sabotaging auctions, refusing to participate in the collection etc.

(2) The decline in the significance of the tithe document itself becomes an object worth studying: by the end of the eighteenth century the tithe had become an 'anachronism', and no longer a reliable basis for the quantitative study of the net product, nor, *a fortiori*, of the gross product: 'the ups and downs of the tithe' rendered it useless 'as an objective index'; a statement we had already formulated in the collective work on fluctuations in the product of the tithe (Goy and Le Roy Ladurie 1972) when we wrote that, at certain periods during the Wars of Religion as in the second half of the eighteenth century, the tithe was no longer valid as an instrument of measurement. The very fact that the tithe did decline in importance has led Nicolas to propose a way of looking at the tithe from a different angle. If we concentrate on the relative importance of the tithe as a social institution, we can catch a glimpse of the underlying human realities. For the tithe represents a kind of 'stake', the product of 'a complex, codified network of conflicting forces, reflecting the interests of each social group in the agricultural world'.

Thus those historians who participated in the two collective surveys and those who have been working individually – despite certain understandable differences and disputes – find they have a common aim: to show how tithe documents, as well as records of ground rents and series of yields, can be used in the analysis of agrarian societies. At the last session of the Paris conference, as at Edinburgh, all the participants expressed a desire to explore this problem in greater depth. I shall attempt to pick out the most thought-provoking suggestions: Ernest Labrousse emphasized the social relevance of studying the variations in prices: 'greater use was made of statistical analysis in the nineteenth century, but it tended to underestimate the real extent of local variations. The curve for each village varied more than that for a larger unit. There was greater variation at the level of the Canton than at the level of the department etc. This applies to variations in prices as well as in production... The shock experienced by the peasant was not the abstract shock of the variation at national level, but what he felt at home. The level at which such research must be conducted is that of the village.'

Was there real progress or growth in the eighteenth century? A question of particular interest to Michel Morineau.

Problems associated with productivity:

Are we dealing with the productivity of labour, capital or the land? (Revel).

The importance of the oscillations in productivity and revenue per capita from one year to the next (Aymard, Goy).

The impossibility of proving our hypotheses so long as we do not have two economic indicators: figures for the productivity of labour, and for the factors affecting reproduction (Bois).

Resistance to the tithe. We should stop counting the number of prosecutions resulting from this but instead work out a typology of resistance; we should study the ingenuity of the peasants faced with disaster, and explain how and why for centuries the tithe remained at a level which was just tolerable (Vincent, Morineau).

The need to investigate the legal and social aspects of the tithe, to explain the long-term trends, but also to assess their social consequences on those involved in production; to draw up a typology of farms and of their social reproduction (Deyon).

The possible directions for research into the significance of the long-term trends in Europe (Guy Bois):

(1) identifying the various trends affecting prices, production and wages, taking into account the 'scissors' effect in the case of agricultural productivity and

industrial productivity; agricultural prices and industrial prices; and prices and wages.

(2) assessing the influence of long-term trends on structures, concentrating especially on the transition from phase A to phase B, since these reflect the nature of the crises and the processes involved in the decline in agricultural productivity.

In short, we would like to issue an invitation for historians to 'complicate' our framework of explanation by providing a more precise analysis of the various trends, by taking social factors into account, by introducing the variable of the productivity of labour and by trying to identify the kinds of model particularly adapted to the different local conditions and to the different socio-economic systems. To do this it is absolutely necessary to continue to compile series of tithes, rents and yields; to extend them to areas where there is a rich but insufficiently explored source of data – in other words, Central and Southern America, Finland and Sweden; to promote research into food consumption from the point of view of supply and demand; to give more attention to the various ways in which the tithe was levied; to draw up a systematic inventory of areas deficient in foodstuffs and to study the fluctuations in the rates of exchange between vegetable products, especially cereals, and animal products or timber; to extend this procedure to areas where there was a considerable food surplus in order to identify the fluctuations in the terms of exchange at a European and intercontinental level; and to concentrate research, for a while, on the organization and production of the small peasant farm and on its relationship to the great estate. This amounts to an immense programme of work, which presupposes new, collective research on the part of historians of agrarian societies all over the world.

PART TWO

Comparative study of trends

EMMANUEL LE ROY LADURIE

WITH THE COLLABORATION OF
MARIE-JEANNE TITS-DIEUAIDE

mυmυmυmυmυmυmυmυmυmυmυmυmυmυmυmυmυmυmυmυmυmυmυmυmυmυmυmυmυmυmυmυmυ.

The end of the Middle Ages: the work of Guy Bois and Hugues Neveux

The pages which follow focus on the history of agricultural production as measured by the tithe. For the methodology of this problem, see the book I edited with Joseph Goy,[1] and the first part of this volume.

Like some other historians, including Baehrel, we started from the idea that because the tithe was a fixed percentage of agricultural production (a tenth, an eleventh etc.), it could be used to measure trends in that production year by year and decade by decade.[2] And so at the conference on tithes in Paris in 1977 we and our collaborators drew up graphs of fluctuations in the product of the tithe in a good many parts of Western and Central Europe, from Spain to Hungary, via France. The period involved runs from the fourteenth to the eighteenth century.

We tried to establish certain trends with the aid not only of the tithe series, but also of documents concerning leases (*fermages*) and ground rents, as well as statistics of agricultural productivity when they existed. In other words, we did our best to describe changes in the gross agricultural product and, where possible, in productivity. In doing this we naturally had to consider other trends; although they were marginal from the point of view of our own research, they still had to be taken into account. For example, we were led to consider changes in the surplus extracted from the peasants by the so-called 'landowning class' (I use this term 'landowning class' in the same sense as the Physiocrats, to include not only the owners of the land but also the clergy, the *seigneurs* and the king as the recipients of

taxes). The surplus was extracted in the form of rent, seigneurial dues, tithes and even in a sense state taxes, although
they will not be considered in the present study. It is also
necessary to take into account underlying population
trends, especially in the countryside, and also the propensity of tithe farmers to pay a high price for the privilege.
This propensity varied not only with the cash they had
available but also with population pressure, which
increased the number of would-be tithe farmers and tended
to raise the level of income from land, whether it took the
form of taxes or rent.[3]

The historian of tithes has to take an overall view of
these trends; to see the interrelations of variables such as
production, rent, wages etc. in order to arrive at the central
objective, which is to estimate the long-term trends in agricultural production. In this general survey I shall mainly be
concerned with the long term (trends of a century or more),
but I shall also deal with periods of a few decades and occasionally with short, dramatic periods of famine and subsistence crisis.

It may be useful to begin from the idea of a long-term
ceiling for agricultural production (or at least the production of cereals), a ceiling which had already been reached
during the first half or the first third of the fourteenth
century before the Black Death. This idea seems to me to be
useful, at least as far as the more populous regions of northern France are concerned. The ceiling was not very much
surpassed until about 1700, or even later.

This idea was put forward by Goy and myself in our
study of 1972. It is supported by some more recent studies
including the work of Neveux on the Cambrésis.[4] In this
region the high level of cereal production which had been
reached during the reign of Philippe le Bel at the beginning
of the fourteenth century was not reached again till the
reign of Louis XVI, and not surpassed till that of Louis-
Philippe in the 1830s! The period between Philippe le Bel
and Louis XVI represents, according to Neveux, a 'long-

term trough'. This 'trough' or depression naturally had its own ups and downs.

In Normandy too, and probably in Picardy, the ceiling of the years 1300 to 1340 is revealed by data concerning not only cereal production but also the land under cultivation and the population.[5] This ceiling in production corresponds to the high level of population (which Pierre Chaunu calls 'le monde plein') of the early fourteenth century in northern France and possibly northern Italy and some parts of Germany as well.[6]

On the other hand, Poland and the countries of central Europe did not reach this level of cereal production; nor were they densely populated around 1300. The 'monde plein' was further to the west.

Now we come to the collapse of the early fourteenth century. There would not be a recovery for a long time – until the 'renaissance' of the sixteenth century. This collapse began, roughly speaking, at the time of the Black Death (1348), but obviously the plague was not solely responsible. In the first half of the fourteenth century, as Postan has shown, demographic pressure was already leading to economic crisis.[7] In the course of the next century – indeed, throughout the late Middle Ages – plague and other epidemics recurred. In France the Hundred Years' War was an economic disaster. As Guy Bois shows, it destroyed agricultural capital, directly or indirectly killed farmers, and spread plague and famine.[8]

This general collapse led to a sharp decline in cereal production by the middle of the fifteenth century. The decline, which reached a very low level before there was a recovery, has been described in terms of different models. The first is the classic French model which I explored in Languedoc and which other writers have since found in the Paris region, Provence, Limagne and Forez. Since then it has been given greater precision by Guy Bois' fine analysis of Normandy. The main elements are the following: a peak in agricultural production towards 1320; a decline by two thirds towards 1450; a rapid recovery from 1460 to 1500. This recovery continued between 1500 and 1560 but lost momentum. In France the cereal production levels of 1320 were reached again – more or less – by 1560. We can speak, therefore, of a reconstitution of the agricultural ecosystem around 1560 on roughly the same scale as before the Black Death. Real income from land and the level of the population declined till about 1450 and then rose again, in parallel with the trend in agricultural production. Despite these broad parallels, there are important variations between these different trends.

Real wages moved in the opposite direction to agricultural production. They rose during the depression of the years 1340 to 1450 and fell again in the period of prosperity which followed. The reason for this is of course the inverse correlation between population and wage trends. When population rises, real wages fall and vice versa. This inverse correlation is valid for Western Europe at least, where the 'stock' of good land is limited.

In Cambrésis the chronology was not very different, except that the recovery of the years 1450–1524 was relatively slow and weak. Declining revenue from the tithe reveals that this area was hit by disaster as a result of the wars raging in the Netherlands and on the north-east frontier of France. This unfortunate episode of the 1480s also affected the Southern Netherlands, corresponding to modern Belgium. In this region the decline of the gross agricultural product towards 1480, cereal production in particular, was accompanied by a trend towards the concentration of holdings into farms somewhat larger than in the past. The trend was a general one, although the chronology varied from place to place. In France the depression of the years 1340 to 1450 was also characterized by a concentration of holdings which may be explained by the drop in population. Conversely, during the Renaissance 'boom', holdings were fragmented, sometimes into very small units, as a result of the growth of population.[9]

Similar trends can be found in the Third World today.

Since case studies are often more illuminating than generalizations, I should like to discuss Upper Normandy and the Cambrésis in rather more detail, following the work of Guy Bois and Hugues Neveux.

In Upper Normandy grain production declined between 1330 and 1450. Recovery began after 1460 and accelerated between 1465 and 1495. During these thirty years grain production increased by 45%, a figure close to the rate of increase of the population in the same period. The race between population and production was on again.[10] Population was in the lead, but production was not far behind, so that living standards were not yet threatened. This recovery shows the remarkable resilience of the economic and social ecosystem.

At the end of the fifteenth century in Normandy the level of agricultural production of the years around 1400 was achieved or regained almost everywhere: in some areas it was even surpassed. Although this level of 1400 was higher than that of 1450, it still remained lower than the high ceilings recorded around 1320 to 1340. These promising results at the very end of the fifteenth century would lead one to hope, then, that around 1550 to 1560, just before the turmoil of the Wars of Religion, Normandy would once again be able to achieve the high level of grain production that she had known around 1300.

We should not, however, compare this recovery, which was typical of the second half of the fifteenth century, with the 'slow but powerful period of growth in the eleventh to the thirteenth centuries'. During this first period land was reclaimed from virtually untouched forests, composed of full-grown trees. In the second half of the fifteenth century, however, it was more a question of clearing undergrowth and bringing land which had already been reclaimed back into cultivation. There had been time for bushes and saplings to re-establish themselves; but the time of troubles had been too short to allow real forests to develop again.

By 1450–1500 the first stages of reclamation were very much in the past (in the eleventh to the thirteenth centuries). It was no longer a question of creating a stock of land but simply of recovering it – of exploiting existing capital. The level of investment in terms of money and labour was therefore much lower than during the great clearances of the Middle Ages. This explains why the period of growth and recovery in the second half of the fifteenth century was so pronounced and so rapid.

After 1500, however, things changed. We can speak of a levelling off, or at least of a deceleration in the rate of growth. Between 1500 and 1550 the Norman tithes which are available to historians were sums paid *in cash* (or, more precisely, the peasants who farmed the tithe paid the clergy in cash, although they had received payment *in kind* from the peasants subject to tithe). According to Bois, these tithes increased three fold in money terms between 1500 and 1550. However, the price of wheat in the same period also increased three fold. In other words, in real terms there was stagnation or a very low increase in the product of the tithe. Agricultural production was increasing more and more slowly, in spite of the considerable increase in population which occurred during this period.

The first tithe strikes, which took place in the sixteenth century, should not be forgotten. These were directly or indirectly inspired by Huguenot ideas which were already having an influence on some peasants at this time. These strikes tended to have an artificially stabilizing effect on the product of the tithe. However, grain production in real terms, as compared with production calculated from the tithes, did clearly level off. The growth rate after 1500 was distinctly slower than it had been during the second half of the fifteenth century.

In Normandy then, as in Languedoc, the 'Malthusian scissors' were opening during the first half or the first two thirds of the sixteenth century (1500 to 1560). There was an ever-increasing gap between the growing population and the level of grain production, which did not keep pace or even remained static. On the other hand, there was not much progress in stockbreeding in France in the sixteenth century either. The outlook was not very bright, and it grew darker still. After 1500 the standard of living of the mass of the population fell in the towns as well as in the country. Agricultural production, especially grain production, lost its elasticity once more. This lack of elasticity was typical of the ecosystem: agricultural production more or less regained the levels it had previously reached in 1300–30, but it could not surpass them.

As far as grain production was concerned, the great depression at the end of the Middle Ages merely led to a temporary decline; it did not result in any permanent changes in agriculture.[11] The ecosystem remained out of balance until the middle of the fifteenth century. After this there was a fairly rapid return to the levels of production reached before the great crisis. These levels remained fairly stable henceforward but the recovery may not always have been complete. We must not, however, underestimate the dramatic decline and enormous fluctuations in grain production (and also in agricultural production in general, and in the population) which took place during the great crisis at the end of the Middle Ages; nor should we fail to take into account the simultaneous increase in real wages, a temporary but semi-recurrent phenomenon.

Following Guy Bois, we can emphasize certain essential points:

(1) the outstanding importance of the fifteenth-century economic and demographic recession, which is without parallel (at least compared with anything that had taken place between 1000 and 1348),

(2) the ecosystem's remarkable powers of recovery (over a few decades),

(3) the numerous correlations between production, population, wages and prices.

All this implies regulating mechanisms which (on this occasion, at least) spring from the movement of population and from the phenomena analysed by Ricardo and Malthus. On this point I am in disagreement with certain Marxist aspects of Guy Bois' model, which in other ways I admire a great deal.

Finally, it is necessary to point out that the picture which has just been drawn is valid not only for Languedoc and Normandy but for other parts of Western Europe as well. The regional monograph is a powerful tool, a case study which reveals the functioning of a whole system in a much larger area.

Another way of studying agricultural production, apart from tithe documents, consists in measuring changes in the amount of land under cultivation. Here are some data concerning eastern Normandy, taken once again from the research of Guy Bois. An examination of the total surface area covered by peasant holdings in a small zone where there was no demesne shows that, in the period 1347–97, 85 to 90% of the land was under cultivation. It is true that some land, perhaps 10% of the sample, went out of cultivation in this period. However, in 1424 the area under cultivation had declined to 58% of the total. Compared with the high level of cultivation before the Black Death there had been a drop of 40%!

Towards 1447–81 only 33% of the land was under cultivation. About two thirds had been abandoned, or a little less, since the land was not cultivated 100% before 1340. However, it should be remembered that Bois is concerned with a small zone of eastern Normandy where the land was almost entirely under cultivation in 'normal' times, that is, before the Black Death and the beginnings of the Hundred Years' War. The forests had long been cleared. In any case the decline of the area under cultivation in this zone was a little less marked than the decline of the population. In the long term, the food situation could improve slightly. Wheat prices therefore remained low during the second half and especially during the third quarter of the fifteenth century, once the war was over. From then on it was possible to enjoy the benefits of the relative abundance of land which could be put back into cultivation.

The situation was all the more favourable towards 1460 in that the marginal and relatively barren land had been abandoned while the good land remained in cultivation. Guy Bois has argued convincingly for this: it was, he wrote, a question of 'a long process of economic and demographic selection'. As the peasants grew less and less numerous in the early fifteenth century, they gradually abandoned the less fertile land on the periphery, and concentrated their efforts on the land in the centre of the village territory which had long been fertilized not only by manure but also by a more intense human effort. In general the decline of the amount of land under cultivation and even the temporary desertion of some villages may be explained simply enough by increased mortality. From a strictly economic point of view, debt contributed to the ruin of the peasantry and led to even more land being abandoned.

In 1474, as the economy began to revive, the amount of land under cultivation expanded, reaching up to 49% of the sample studied. Recovery was complete by 1526 with between 90 and 95% of all land under cultivation, much as it had been in the fourteenth century. Virtually all marginal land had now been taken into cultivation.

The final phase of reoccupation was accompanied by a considerable increase in ground rent and in the price of land. These two series of data may be used by the historian as relevant but indirect indices which help us to understand why more land was taken into cultivation and agricultural production increased. At the beginning of the economic revival, between 1446 and 1475, ground rent and the price of land remained stable. However, in Normandy the price of land increased almost three and a half times in nominal terms between 1470 and 1508–9, at a time when there was little or no increase in the price of wheat. Thus the crucial phases of both agricultural recovery and the increase in the demand for land took place roughly between 1475 and 1505. One is struck once again by the violence of the ups and downs of the cyclical process (lasting 200 years) in which land went in and out of cultivation. These oscillations are 'correlated with the regulatory mechanisms of the economy' and are generally concerned with production, real wages, rent and the fragmentation of holdings in proportion to the rise in population. There is also a correlation with the regulatory mechanisms of the ecosystem: the good land was the last to be abandoned towards 1440 and the first to be brought back into cultivation towards 1470. Conversely, the poor lands were the first to be abandoned and the last to be reclaimed.

I come now to the model of Hugues Neveux which relates to the Cambrésis from 1330 to 1830 (Neveux 1980). Neveux has taken a sample of 7,070 hectares (17,463 acres), or about 14% of the 51,000 hectares of the Cambrésis. Neveux is concerned to study production trends via the tithe and also to place them in their economic and social framework; he does not avoid the methodological problems we have already discussed. According to him the farmer's profit is approximately 10–20% of the tithe he collected: in other words, the tithe informs us about 85% of the trend in the gross product of the grain subject to it. In the Cambrésis the tithe also indicates the changing percentages of the different cereals grown. For example the oat crop declined relative to wheat between 1360 and 1600. The proportion changed from 1.5 oats to 1 wheat in 1360 to 0.9 oats to 1 wheat in 1600. The lower classes adopted wheat bread instead of porridge and the demand for oats therefore declined. The price of oats in the Cambrésis increased much less than the price of wheat between 1375 and 1630; the annual rate of increase in the price of oats in those two and a half centuries was only 77% of the rate for wheat.

Neveux presents a series of indices of the production of

cereals (corn + oats + barley) in the Cambrésis. (Base year 1370 = 100.)

- around 1320 index 145–150
- around 1370 index 100
- around 1450–1460 index 75
- around 1520–1540 index 85
- around 1610–1620 index 75
- around 1700 index 100
- around 1750 index 110
- around 1780 index 150
- around 1840 index 165

It is therefore easy to pick out the long-term trends of the agricultural ecosystem, by looking at the particular trend in the Cambrésis (see Figure 3). According to Neveux:

(a) the whole of the period from 1370 to 1750 was one of relative economic depression, when one compares it with the high level of cereal production recorded at the beginning of the fourteenth century and again at the end of the eighteenth century and the beginning of the nineteenth. This is what Neveux refers to as the 'long-term trough'.

(b) In the long term there were some very considerable oscillations in cereal production. For example:

- a period of continuous recession from 1370 to 1455;
- a period of recuperation from 1460 to 1530;
- a period of stagnation or even recession from 1550 to the beginning of the seventeenth century.

(c) Finally, in the eighteenth century there was a sharp increase in production which amounted to a full recovery. A similar process took place in other areas of northern France, for example the extreme north, especially the area around Lille (according to the studies of Deyon and his students). There were therefore high ceilings at each end of this period, in the fourteenth century and again in the eighteenth. In between these extremes there was a long-term depression or a localized 'trough' which was especially evident during the seventeenth century. Throughout this

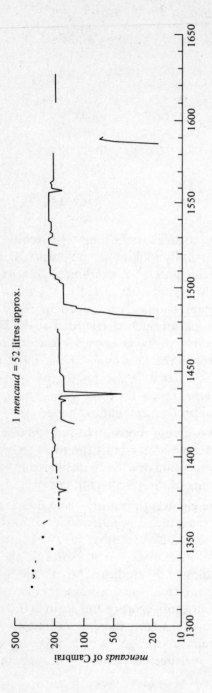

1 *mencaud* = 52 litres approx.

3. Tithe and *terrage* in the Cambrésis, 1320–1630 (H. Neveux, *Les grains du Cambrésis*, Paris, 1980, pp. 62–3)

period any short-term periods of recovery such as the one from 1455–60 to 1500 had little effect. These short-term improvements only made a serious difference during the eighteenth century when, during the Louis XVI period, the high levels of cereal production achieved at the time of Philippe le Bel (1300–30) were at last reached again. This very early period of high grain production – at a time, it is true, when there was an enormous population to consume it – was not really to be matched again until the age of Louis-Philippe, in 1830 to 1840. But it is true that the last period of growth or 'supergrowth' in the eighteenth and nineteenth centuries in the Cambrésis coincided with changes in the agrarian structure.

To return to the 1320s, the high production of cereals which characterized the Cambrésis at this time can be partially explained by high demand resulting from the very large population. It can also be explained by the practice of agricultural techniques which enabled cultivation to be extremely intensive for the period. Neveux mentions in particular the cultivation of rape (for oil), and of peas and beans on part of the fallow every third year. After the crisis of the years 1340–50 these intensive techniques were gradually abandoned. This is one explanation for the beginning of the long-term decline in cereal production. Much later, in the second half of the eighteenth century, a new, intensive system was established nearly four centuries after the previous one had disappeared. The second system was different from the first, which is not surprising given how much time had elapsed between the two. The new system, which was established between 1750 and 1850, was based on the cultivation of flax, clover, sainfoin and colza on the fallow land. This was a late imitation of Dutch and Flemish techniques which had been developed in the north since the Renaissance. Other factors also contributed to the improvement of agriculture in the Cambrésis, such as a denser pattern of sowing, new types of plough and the use of ash as a fertilizer.

Meanwhile, from roughly 1350 to the early years of the eighteenth century, after the end of the first phase of intensive agriculture and before the establishment of the second, there was a general lack of technological innovation in this region, especially so far as tools were concerned. Agricultural production in the Cambrésis relied on fertile soil, a climate favourable to grain, and agricultural techniques which, even if they did not develop, appeared to be relatively efficient from the fourteenth/fifteenth centuries onwards. These techniques were capable of dealing with different or unexpected conditions, so that no urgent need was felt for a breakthrough in agricultural technology. Traditional but not inefficient, the agriculture of the Cambrésis was not stretched to the limit – if necessary, it was capable of limited growth without any need for major technological changes. It responded to the rises and falls of population and demand by increasing or decreasing the amount produced. In short, it was flexible. After reading Neveux's work, it is difficult to know what to think of the striking ideas of Morineau,[12] according to whom agricultural yields remained fixed and stable in France from the end of the Middle Ages to the nineteenth century. In fact, the last phase of growth or strong recovery in the Cambrésis between 1660 and 1780 was the result of an *increase* in cereal yields from 12 hectolitres to the hectare to 19 or 20. This tends to prove that yields were far from being totally stable in the long term. The sample used by Neveux was more reliable. It covered 7,000 hectares, whereas Morineau worked on a mere 140 hectares, in the extreme north of France – which more or less amounts to studying the weather of a vast region from a small garden in the suburbs. In a sense, however, we have to admit that Morineau is not completely wrong. The increase in yields in the Cambrésis in the eighteenth century was indeed a very slow recovery; after the long trough, these yields returned to or exceeded the peak they had reached at the beginning of the fourteenth century.

In any case, Neveux and Morineau do not always dis-
agree. In the most fertile regions of the extreme north of
France both men have found a number of instances
throughout the whole period of cereal yields which are
higher than 15 hectolitres to the hectare and not far below
18. These instances cluster in the most favourable – or least
unfavourable – periods. However, Neveux had shown that
in this fertile 'extreme north' of France these high yields
coexisted with a whole spectrum of average and low ones.
The long-term fluctuations of the 'average yield' corresponded to an expansion or a contraction of this spectrum,
according to the period. This pattern accounts for a large
part of the positive or negative trends in cereal production
at different periods.

Thus the yield levels in the Cambrésis varied between 10
and 21 hectolitres to the hectare around 1320. In this
period there was a large population and a numerous workforce which could weed the fields without difficulty, thanks
to the participation of women and many children – hence
there were very high yields. Towards 1450 yields varied
between 4 and 18 hectolitres to the hectare: this was the
phase of depression. Towards 1520 there was a partial recovery and yields varied between 10 and 18 hectolitres to
the hectare, but towards 1625 they fell again to between 6
and 18. These fluctuations occurred for the most part on
marginal lands. These lands were badly cultivated during
long-term periods of depression (for example towards
1625), and at the worst moments (towards 1450) sometimes went out of cultivation altogether.

These long-term trends on the supply side are linked to
fluctuations in the demand for cereals. In the Cambrésis
this could have been affected by external demand, from the
Netherlands for example. Was this an important factor? In
the fifteenth century and in the first half of the sixteenth
century up to 10% of the grain was exported to the Spanish
Netherlands and even to the Dutch Republic. After 1550
grain from the Baltic competed for the Netherlands

market, and in the end the Cambrésis more or less lost this traditional outlet.

However, the ebb and flow of cereal production in the Cambrésis chiefly depended on the fluctuations in the *domestic* demand. They also depended to a considerable extent on local population trends. More generally, foreign and domestic demand was a function of population trends in a zone including the present territory of Belgium as well as the north of France.

Guy Bois and Hugues Neveux both suggest a correlation between tithe and cereal production trends and 'human productivity' (a concept not to be confused with that of the productivity of the soil). In the Cambrésis (and in Normandy) towards 1320 land was scarce and labour was abundant, thanks to overpopulation. Human productivity was low; one can talk of low marginal productivity of labour. In 1450 it was the reverse – land was abundant, labour was scarce, so human productivity and the marginal productivity of labour were high, and as a result real wages were also high.

In this context the word 'productivity' takes on a rather special meaning: the changes which affected it were not linked to technical changes, as was the case when one considers the increase in productivity per hectare during the twentieth century. Paradoxically, the high level of cereal production around 1320 was accompanied by low human (or marginal) productivity; conversely the low levels of grain production around 1450 correspond to a period of high human or marginal productivity. This special meaning of productivity essentially expresses the relationship between the availability of land on one side and labour on the other, without implying any technological progress.

Rents in the Cambrésis – as in Normandy and in the Hurepoix – fluctuated roughly in line with trends in grain production and in the scarcity or abundance of land. When production was high and land scarce, around 1320–40, rents were high; conversely they dropped during periods of low grain production when there was plenty of fallow land available (around 1450).

So far, with regard to the Cambrésis, I have only considered long-term trends. But in addition to annual, or short-term changes, there were intermediate ten-year trends referred to by Hugues Neveux. They were not provoked by the same factors as the long-term changes which, as we have seen, were essentially bound up with slow changes in yields, which were themselves in the last analysis determined by fluctuations in demand – external or internal – which were in turn closely connected with the overall changing levels of population in the Cambrésis and the vast area around it.

The ten-year slumps, on the other hand, may be correlated with the decline of the area under cultivation as a result of devastation caused by war and, at times, epidemics – in other words, with subsistence crises of one kind or another. Some of these slumps even exceeded the ten-year framework and spilled over into long-term rather than medium-term trends. This was the case, for example, in the Cambrésis in 1340–50. In the early 1340s there was a period of crisis resulting from war devastation; plagues broke out in 1348 and transformed an already serious situation into a widespread decline in population, which led in turn to a decline in grain production and a shortage of food for those surviving. This period of disasters lasted more than a decade and was to lead, in turn, to a long-term depression. This began in the 1350s; its basic characteristics were those of the very long-term trend in cereal production in the Cambrésis during the fourteenth and fifteenth centuries; it marked the beginning of the 'long-term trough' which stretched in this area from the fourteenth century to the eighteenth century. The slump of the 1340s represented, as we have seen, the beginning of the decline of the old intensive agriculture which had been characteristic of the Cambrésis throughout the first half of the fourteenth century.

Later on, we can pick out crisis periods of approximately ten years in 1415–27, 1476–83 (subsistence crises, war and all their consequences), 1523–30, and 1553–60. These crises interrupted the long-term trends; they could amount to a decline in production of 25% or more. Their causes were often specific – for example they took place in the border regions between France and the Netherlands as a result of the wars in this area. There is no contemporary equivalent of these trends on actual *French* territory at this period: 1480 and 1550 were in fact absorbed into a relatively favourable trend, around Paris or Montpellier.

On the other hand, certain very severe crises temporarily reduced the tithes in the Cambrésis between 1580 and 1590 (during our Wars of Religion). The same thing happened again in the second third of the seventeenth century (between 1635 and 1659), during the Thirty Years' War. These two periods of slump were well in line with the general trend in France, especially in northern France, a region into which the Cambrésis was more and more integrated from an economic point of view during the sixteenth and seventeenth centuries.

Between 1560 and 1660 the Cambrésis was thus completely involved in the seventeenth-century depression. This depression was the result of common European factors which amount to what has commonly been described as the 'general crisis of the seventeenth century'. It was, however, provoked more immediately by wars which were specifically French (Wars of Religion, the Thirty Years' War and the Fronde). The Thirty Years' War, of course, differed from the Wars of Religion in that it did not only involve France; Germany and Spain were also affected.

The longer slumps of 1580–1600 and 1635–59 in the Cambrésis reduced the volume of tithes and to some extent that of agricultural production. This reduction could reach 35 to 40 or even 50%; whereas the similar slumps which had taken place in 1415 to 1560 had resulted in the Cambrésis in a reduction in the tithe of not more than 25%.

This deterioration seems to have been the result of 'progress' in the art of war. The permanent armies, which were well established at the end of the sixteenth and especially in the seventeenth century, were distinctly more dangerous than the soldiers of the fifteenth and the first half of the sixteenth centuries. However, we must not overgeneralize. In Normandy in 1420–45 Guy Bois talks of a 'Hiroshima model'.

After 1660–70 a period of steady growth began in the Cambrésis – this was the beginning of the large-scale recovery over a long period which was to mark the eighteenth century. This period of stability – which from then on was not punctuated by any major slump – was in itself a source of relative well-being; it represented a certain form of progress in the age of the Enlightenment.

It is possible to pick out certain links between long-term changes and periods of decline lasting one or possibly two decades. The short-term slumps aggravated, initiated or altered the course of the long-term depressions. The short- and medium-term slumps themselves, however, were invariably connected with war. This was a more important factor than the weather: it is true that a poor harvest resulting from rain or frost could intensify a short-term slump, but even if this pattern recurred the following year it would not by itself cause any lasting damage. How are we to explain this crucial rôle of war as a cause of slumps in the gross agricultural product over a period of one or more decades? It seems likely that a prejudice against the importance formerly attributed to battles may have led us to underestimate the importance of war itself. Historians may safely forget the odd *battle*; but they cannot construct viable explanations without taking *wars* into account.

Wars destroyed agricultural capital, they spread insecurity, and they prevented the peasants from ploughing and harvesting for fear of being attacked by soldiers. The major difference between disasters provoked by the climate and those provoked by war was that the latter continued all year – or for several years – without remission. Thus the effects of war on agricultural production tended to be cumulative. During the wars of the mid-sixteenth century the harvests in the Cambrésis were destroyed or damaged by the passage of troops in 1552, 1553, 1554, 1555 and 1557. The only year free from war was 1556, but unfortunately this year coincided with a severe drought whose effects were felt as far away as England. After the wars had ended and the armies were no longer roaming the countryside it took several years to repair the damage caused to the economy and to agricultural production. This was the way out of the slump – until the next one.

Between the sixteenth and the eighteenth centuries the ecosystem in the Cambrésis slowly recovered the impressive economic and demographic levels it had attained before the Black Death. But this process (which included the gradual recovery of the previous levels of grain production) was not merely a matter of restoring the past. The agricultural ecosystem itself underwent certain changes of a capitalist, or at least seigneurial type. Between the fifteenth and the seventeenth centuries, a network of large farms was established (large by French standards, at least: what the French call a large farm would often be considered a medium-sized one in Britain).

There remains the problem of explaining the long stagnation of cereal production at a relatively low level in the Cambrésis in the sixteenth and seventeenth centuries. To clear up the mystery, Neveux studied the large farms, which were oriented towards the market, rather than the small ones, which aimed rather at self-sufficiency. According to Neveux, the large farms (50, 60 or 100 acres) were responsible for half the gross cereal product in the Cambrésis in this period, and more than half the cereals which were sold on the open market.

In the sixteenth century, the large farms became more and more of a grain factory. The permanent workforce maintained a fairly high level of productivity. At peak periods the necessary extra workers were recruited by the day and dismissed when there was no more need for them. However, after 1550 the large farm (known as the *cense*) in the Cambrésis did not try to keep up with the rising population by increasing its grain production in proportion. The *cense* did not drag the tithes of the Cambrésis out of their long-term trough. In these circumstances it is necessary to ask why the large farmers of the area did not show more entrepreneurial drive.

One possible answer is that they were exploited by the 'landowning class' which took 40% of the gross product of the farm in the form of rents, tithes and heavy seigneurial dues, like *terrage* or *champart*. It is certainly true that the large landowners reinvested only 20% of their revenues in their land. However, the rise in rents in the first half of the sixteenth century was more than cancelled out for the substantial tenant farmers by the decline in the real wages they paid their farm hands. It is well known that real wages declined during the Renaissance. Nevertheless, Neveux does not over-emphasize this explanation in terms of wages. He offers a psychological explanation of the lack of entrepreneurial drive: if the economic performance of the substantial tenant farmers was mediocre it was because they did not behave in the manner of *homo economicus*. In short, these gentlemen did not make the best of the opportunities offered to them and did not increase the productivity of their farms.

Is this psychological explanation relevant? Let us at any rate agree that French cereal production in the regions studied in recent theses seldom surpassed the 1320–30 level in the course of the sixteenth and seventeenth centuries.

In the course of this chapter I have drawn heavily on the work of Neveux and Bois. I shall now say something more general about France (north and south) during the crises of the fourteenth and fifteenth centuries.

Comparative study of trends

In the Paris region the revenue which the Church obtained from its lands declined in *real* terms by 66% between 1340 and 1420. The amount produced must therefore have declined by at least 50%.

In the south (in Forez and Provence) we are only able to compare the tithe levels of the 1430s with those of the end of the fifteenth century, a time when cereal production was already beginning to recover. In this case, too, the level of 1420 was only 40% of what it would be in the 1490s.

It therefore seems reasonable to suggest that cereal production declined by 50% or more between the 1330s and (say) the second quarter of the fifteenth century. Since the population declined still more (possibly by as much as two thirds), there was more grain available per head in the 1450s (when peace returned) than there had been in the 1330s. In other words, although grain production declined in absolute terms, the population declined still further.

6

The recovery of the sixteenth century

In the sixteenth century, in sharp contrast with the previous period, there is a remarkable consistency amongst those countries for which we have tithe data. There was expansion and growth almost everywhere, at least in the period 1500 to 1560 or 1570. This is not, of course, a new discovery. Historians have spoken of the 'splendid' sixteenth century as a time of significant economic and demographic expansion. Despite this general trend, however, there was considerable poverty at an individual level because the increase in food production did not keep pace with the increase in population.[1] The uniformity of agricultural expansion from Poland to Spain was very striking; it was not to be repeated during the second period of growth which began in the eighteenth century.

Needless to say, to refer to the sixteenth century as 'splendid' is to use superficial, metaphorical language. In fact the population increased more rapidly than production, which led to impoverishment, at least so far as real wages and the per capita income of the peasants were concerned. These phenomena were not particularly 'splendid', but rather were 'harsh'.

I shall begin with central Europe; my first chapter was essentially concerned with France, as I did not have enough data for other countries in the fourteenth and fifteenth centuries, but I can now widen my scope.

First, let us look at Poland in the sixteenth century. The studies of Topolski and Wyczanski for the 1977 Conference[2] on cereal production in Poland did not draw on evidence from the tithe, but they were able to establish the main trend on the basis of other sources. The concept of a 'long-term ceiling' for cereal production does not seem to be particularly relevant. The sixteenth century was a period of real growth in Poland, it was not simply a matter of re-covering previous levels of production (as was often the case in France, especially for grain). Expansion reached its peak in Poland around 1560–70. This was the classic Euro-pean pattern. In this period, Poland, like Hungary, was in step with Western Europe as far as agricultural production was concerned. The second peak in Polish grain production was to occur around 1790, after the crisis of the second half of the seventeenth century and after the partial recovery of the eighteenth century. This time, though, it was to reach only about 90% of the 1560–70 level – which makes the sixteenth-century achievement all the more remarkable.

In Hungary, excellent tithe series have been discovered

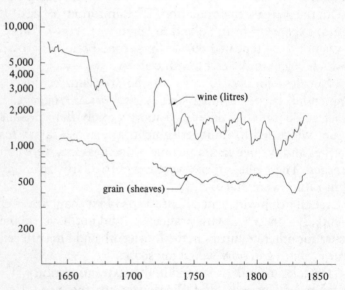

4. Wine and grain production in Rust, Hungary, 1630–1850 (Makkai and Zimanyi)

by Hunyadi, Kiss, Makkai and Mrs Zimanyi.[3] They have analysed them with the help of a computer. The tithes reveal a high level of production for wine, wheat and grain in general throughout the sixteenth century, especially when one compares these high levels with the long-term depression which set in during the seventeenth century; the levels were also higher than those of the eighteenth century. In the region studied by Kiss, grain production in 1660 had fallen to 40% of its level in 1550–60. These sixteenth-century tithes were not equalled in Hungary until about 1820. The decline can be interpreted in a number of ways: between the sixteenth and the seventeenth centuries there was a decrease in grain production, but there was also a decline in population.

We do not yet have much data for Germany. It is to be hoped that this situation will change since Swiss researchers, like Mme Head-Koenig, have shown that there is plenty of material on tithes in German-speaking countries – Switzerland, Germany itself, and Austria. Before coming on to Switzerland, I should like to mention the Netherlands, another important region bordering onto the Germanies.

For the Netherlands I have used the studies of Van der Wee and Van Cauwenberghe on agricultural income, the tithe and 'farms' (for which a landlord sold the right to collect his rents).[4] They obtained these figures from the records of ecclesiastical institutions and hospitals in what is now Belgium and the Netherlands. These data emphasize that the sixteenth century was a period of significant growth. Mme Tits believes that this period saw an increase in the productivity of the land (as a result of the intensification of human labour by technological and other means) between the fifteenth and the sixteenth centuries. This should not be confused with what Guy Bois calls the productivity per head of the peasant, which depends only on a correlation between the rural population and the amount of land under cultivation (see the previous chapter). The in-

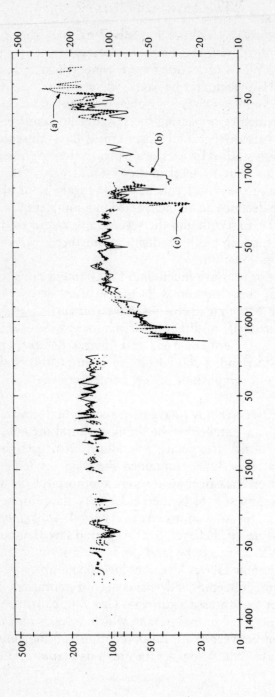

5. Grain tithes in south-western Brabant, 1400–1770 (F. Daelemans in Van der Wee (1978), p. 35. Reprinted by permission of Louvain University Press)

(a) = Leerbeek   (b) = Pepingen   (c) = average   1402–3 = 100

tensification of agriculture in the Netherlands in the sixteenth century was to be of lasting benefit in the next few centuries of the *ancien régime*.

Was the growth in production and in productivity in the Netherlands in the sixteenth century merely (as was often the case in France) a matter of returning to the high levels of production of the fourteenth century, before the Black Death? Did this recovery begin after the long depression of 1350 to 1450?

The answer to this question is probably no. As Van der Wee points out: 'In the Netherlands agricultural productivity did not follow the same course as in France. The high levels reached at the beginning of the fourteenth century were not followed by a catastrophic collapse – on the whole, a reasonable level of productivity was maintained throughout the European depression of the fourteenth and fifteenth centuries. In the sixteenth century there was even an upward turn which exceeded the levels of the 1300s. This improvement continued throughout the seventeenth century, especially in the coastal areas of the Northern Netherlands (now Holland). In the eighteenth century new records were achieved in the Southern Netherlands (now Belgium), thanks to a rapid increase in the diversification of crops. Thus, the agricultural revolution began in the Netherlands in the sixteenth and productivity rose almost continuously from that date.'[5] The agricultural revolution which began in the Netherlands in the sixteenth century moved in an anti-clockwise direction from the countryside of Antwerp and Amsterdam, towards England in the seventeenth and eighteenth centuries, and to France in the eighteenth and especially the nineteenth centuries.

There was a distinct increase in grain yields in the Netherlands in the sixteenth century. Yields of rye, barley and oats, so far as is known, were 11, 32 and 71% higher respectively in 1502–1726 than they had been in the fifteenth century.[6] 'This increase in productivity would be even more pronounced if one took into account not the whole period 1502–1726, but just the sixteenth century.'

However, the Netherlands in the sixteenth century did not prosper merely because of high cereal yields. 'In the sixteenth century the rise in population and the fairly rapid urbanization of the Netherlands helped productivity to increase not just in physical terms but also in terms of value.[7] Massive imports of grain from the Baltic via Holland meant that agriculture in the coastal and urban zones could concentrate on specialized, diversified crops; these gave the peasants a better return because they were in demand on the urban markets and because the land and the available labour force could be used more rationally. Holland and Friesland concentrated on dairy products. Groningen, Overijssel and Drenthe specialized more in livestock. In northern and western Brabant and in Flanders horticulture and hops were widespread. In Flanders and Zeeland there was an increase in flax growing. This gave rise to weaving and spinning industries and helped to wipe out a great deal of "hidden unemployment" in various rural areas. It was precisely this optimum combination of agriculture with cottage industries, especially in the flax-growing and linen-weaving sector, that caused the rents and prices of agricultural land to rise noticeably in southeast Flanders until about 1580.' In any case, a comparison between the good results of 1530–50 with the less happy decades of the second half of the fifteenth century in the Lier and west Brabant regions reveals (in the case of tithes and various forms of income in kind or calculated in real terms) increases varying between 15 and 50%, averaging out at about 33%.

This increase in the revenues extracted from the peasantry (tithes, 'farms' etc.) was not the result (so the Belgian historians tell us)[8] of another 'turn of the screw' by the proprietors at the expense of their farmers. It was rather the result of investment, technological progress, a rise in productivity and a diversification in the crops produced.

The sixteenth century

This increase in prosperity cannot be called capitalist. It was the small farms which prospered, producing not only enough to feed the farmer and his family but a surplus for the market as well. These small farms were subdivided still further during the first half of the fifteenth century, a time when the population was already increasing again, at least in the Netherlands (unlike France). In the period which followed, demographic decline and economic crisis had the opposite effect, and holdings became concentrated again, so as to form larger farms on the average between 1450 and 1500. This is not to say that really large estates were formed: the family farm was still dominant. The third stage, after 1500, saw another rise in population leading to another round of subdivision. Between 1500 and 1550 there was a proliferation of small farms averaging between 1.5 and 3.75 hectares (4 to 9.5 acres). Finally, between 1550 and 1580, division went still further and tiny farms from 0.75 and 1.5 hectares (2 to 4 acres) multiplied. These results are extremely different from those of Georges Frêche, according to whom an increase in population does not lead to the subdivision of peasant holdings. In fact there is a correlation between the two phenomena, whether we are talking about the Netherlands or Languedoc in the sixteenth century, or the Third World today. However, even when the population is increasing, it is possible for capitalists to concentrate holdings as in the case of the Toulouse area or, still more obviously, England in the eighteenth century.[9]

In the Netherlands, in the absence of rural large-scale capitalism, an increase in population was indeed followed by a subdivision of holdings, and also by an increase in agricultural productivity in the course of the sixteenth century. This allows us to qualify certain slightly too definite statements by Brenner.[10] According to him, the only way for agriculture to modernize was to pass through the English stage of large estates with advanced technology, However, the example of the Netherlands shows that there is more than one path to agricultural improvement. One way to improve was that of the large, English-style farm, but at an earlier stage the rôle of the small yet efficient Flemish family farm was an important one.

In the Netherlands between 1500 and 1550 there were several simultaneous developments which enabled the peasant family to exploit a smaller farm than in the past, without any reduction in their standard of living. These factors consisted of an increase in agricultural production, a growth in population, technological progress, a movement towards cultural diversification, the subdivision of farms and the development of rural industries. These phenomena are reflected or refracted by increases in the tithe, 'farms' and in other forms of revenue from the land.

In England, according to D. C. Coleman, wheat yields increased by 30% between 1450 and 1650.[11] However, it was largely after 1650 that Dutch techniques became established in England, so this factor accounts only in part for the English agricultural revolution – purely local improvements in technology and agronomy were also important. In the sixteenth century England was an intermediate case, somewhere between the qualitatively new type of agricultural growth to be found in the Netherlands on the one hand, and on the other, the French trend towards the simple restoration or reproduction of the old medieval ecosystem of the period before the disasters of 1340–1450. In France this 'old model' often persisted without serious modification throughout the economic renaissance of 1460–1560.

Grain yields in France do not appear to have inreased very much in the sixteenth century, compared with the Middle Ages. What had happened to cereal production? I shall study this question by looking at the tithe, and by examining, with some caution, the fluctuations in the level of rents, or 'farms'. Around Paris the curves obtained from these various indices (expressed in real terms) began to rise again, after the disastrous crisis of 1420–40. From a base-

line of 100 in 1450–70, these curves reached or even exceeded 200 (still calculating in real terms). This was
essentially a recovery of the high levels which had already
been recorded before the Black Death and the Hundred
Years' War. However, it is not clear that cereal output
around Paris and in Normandy at the end of the renaissance (around 1560) had completely returned to the highest
levels of the pre-plague period (around 1300 to 1340).[12]

There were two distinct phases in this process of recovery:

(a) The first phase was one of rapid reconstruction
between 1450 and 1500. In these fifty years agricultural
income almost doubled, in real terms.

(b) The second phase was marked by a slowing down in
the rate of growth. The levels remained high, and were still
rising, but the curve was flattening out. Cereal production
was reaching the ceilings of the early modern period. This
second phase revealed a decline in the rate of the recovery
of agriculture from 1500 onwards, which occurred at a
time when the population continued to increase rapidly.
This situation led to numerous subsistence crises around
Paris and in France in general in 1520–35. However, the
years 1540 to 1560, immediately preceding the Wars of Religion, appear to have been relatively prosperous: one has
the impression that the peasants made a final effort to feed
a population which would in future become too numerous
for them.

In the south of France – in Limagne, Forez, Languedoc
and Provence – we have data for the fluctuations in the
tithe and for grain production. The overall pattern in these
areas was not very different from the Paris region and from
northern France. In other words:

– a phase of steady recovery, which possibly began a
little earlier than in the north, sometimes from 1430 on (in
the Auvergne);

– a slowing down in the rate of growth between 1500
and 1560, when production was nearing a type of Malthus-

ian ceiling. This ceiling was reached around 1560, and in many cases was not to be exceeded – at least as far as grain production was concerned – until the eighteenth or even the nineteenth century.

The subsistence crises of the years 1520–33, especially towards 1529, are obvious in the south of France as well. They were the result of an excess of rainfall and also to the fact that it was not possible to produce enough grain to keep up with the growing population. The northern French model is thus applicable in the south as well:

- recovery 1450–1500, or even 1430–1500;
- decline in the rate of growth, 1500–60;
- short-term subsistence crises, around 1527–33.

The discovery of unpublished data and the construction of new curves for the Beauce and Normandy has not modified this northern model, which seems to fit the south as well.[13]

In the case of a number of French regions data for the late Middle Ages are lacking and so it is impossible to compare the growth of the sixteenth century with the depression of the fifteenth century. However, in France as in Hungary, it is possible to compare the sixteenth century with the seventeenth. From this point of view, too, the sixteenth century represents a 'ceiling'. In Alsace, for example, the grain tithes of 1560–83 were 90% of what they would be during the happy period of 1600–30, before the terrible impact, *circa* 1630–50, of the Thirty Years' War.

The same conclusion is valid for Burgundy and Languedoc, where the level reached in the best decades of the seventeenth century was virtually the same as that of 1540–60. It is true that in Burgundy the development of wine-growing in the centuries which followed increased the total income of the region, although cereal production stagnated. The same is true of Languedoc, where wine-growing developed in certain zones during the seventeenth century and still more in the eighteenth century.

To return to the northern French model of stable cereal production. In Switzerland, too, which it is convenient to treat in this case as if it were part of France, cereal yields were high in the sixteenth century and were not to surpass this level in the following centuries.[14] The grain tithe reached its peak around 1550 in Switzerland, as elsewhere in Western Europe, and it remained at this level during the seventeenth century and sometimes during the eighteenth century as well.

So far as the relation between the supply of and the demand for cereals is concerned, it is useful to divide the period 1450–1560 into two parts:

(1) From 1450 to 1500 or 1505. The increase in the grain supply kept pace with the growth of population and in some cases even overtook it. The terrible famines of the Hundred Years' War were a thing of the past. There was a good deal of land available which could be brought back into cultivation and made to produce grain without much effort or expense. The period was one of relative abundance, without famine and with only a few shortages, a few bumps on the curve of grain prices. Serious subsistence crises were no more than a memory, or a premonition of a future which was only beginning to appear on the horizon.

(2) From about 1505 to 1520, cereal production increased only slowly. Diminishing returns began to set in, while the population continued to increase, especially in the towns, which now contained a higher percentage of the French population than they had done in the past, even if this large percentage remained a low one in absolute terms.

Generally speaking, the supply of grain was sufficient to meet demand. However, a famine or a serious shortage was inevitable whenever weather conditions were bad, as in the case of the heavy rains of the 1520s and early 1530s, the drought of 1556 in France and in England, the freezing weather of the 1690s or the terrible winter of 1709. The danger of famine ceased to be serious at an earlier date in England than in France. In England the last subsistence crisis seems to have occurred in the 1620s, and in Scotland in the 1690s. In France, however, in the great grain-growing region of the Paris Basin, subsistence crises did not disappear till after the year 1740. One reason for their disappearance was the increase in cereal production, another was the fact that communication had been improved and stone barns had been built, thus making it easier to store grain when times were good and to transport it when times were bad.

To return to the sixteenth century. The price of grain was necessarily influenced by the slowing down in the growth of production at a time when population was continuing to increase. This is particularly noticeable during subsistence crises such as the 1520s, when there were some temporary peaks on the graph of wheat prices. There were also some longer-term effects. Between 1510 and 1580, cereal prices increased much more than those of other foods. For example, wheat prices in Paris rose by 120% between 1510 and 1540 while the price of wine and mutton in the same period rose by only 41%.[15] This differential became still sharper in the Paris region between 1540 and 1560. There were three reasons for the discrepancy:

(1) Increased demand for grain, thanks to the rise in population and the urban expansion between 1500 and 1560.

(2) The slowing down in the rate of increase in the supply of grain over the same period. The years 1560–80 were characterized by 'stagflation' (stagnation of production accompanied by a persistent inflation).

· (3) An increase in the 'marginal cost of production and trade' as a result of taking poorer land into cultivation and of an increase in the cost of transporting grain. What was happening was that the towns, with their increasing population, needed more and more cereals which consequently had to be brought longer and longer distances over roads which remained bad or virtually non-existent. There was no substitute for grain, for the age of maize and potatoes had not yet arrived. Cereal prices therefore rose more rapidly than those of other agricultural products between

1510 and 1580. Until 1540 they increased faster than the prices of industrial goods. In other words, the supply of good land suitable for cereal production could not be increased very much.

However, cereals are not the only factor, either in France or the Netherlands. What about other agricultural products? The question is the same as that already asked in the case of the Netherlands, but the answer will be different. There is also a danger of this answer being incomplete and more qualitative than quantitative. In Mediterranean France some fairly important olive plantations were established between 1500 and 1570. The vines of Languedoc did not increase noticeably during this period, but there was a certain increase in such production on the east and west banks of the Rhône valley, even if it was not yet all that important in terms of the amount and value of what was produced.

In the south-west the production of woad increased considerably. This dye-stuff was first required by the Spanish textile industry and was imported from the area around Toulouse via Burgos. From 1510 to 1530 the demand for woad increased in the north (Flanders, England and Normandy). The area around Toulouse remained an important source of production but the woad was now transported via the Garonne and the port of Bordeaux. Woad production developed around 1530–60 in a huge rectangle 40 kilometres long and 20 kilometres wide in the clay to the south and south-east of Toulouse. In the first half of the sixteenth century this woad from Aquitaine was extremely successful; it was marketed by the great Toulouse merchants, like Bernuy and Assezat, between 1540 and 1561. In the next forty years, however, the Wars of Religion had a damaging effect on woad production; and later on the French woad suffered severely from the competition of indigo from the tropics. The Wars of Religion (1560–95) damaged woad production around Toulouse by interfering with trade routes and by hampering the harvesting and the storage of the crop. Moreover, during these forty years woad production increased in southern England, as traditional French sources of supply dried up.[16] What is more, woad was seen as a luxury product: peasants in Normandy at this period refused to wear clothes dyed with woad.[17] The economy expands when it is stimulated by an increase in demand for goods for mass consumption: this was not the case for woad.

In the seventeenth century the very same region around Toulouse which had produced woad went over to maize. This was to have important consequences, since from then on the peasant diet was based on maize, and wheat was released for export.

Another non-cereal crop in central and Mediterranean France and in the Latin countries was the vine. This may surprise the English reader, since in Great Britain wine was seen almost entirely as a luxury item. In Mediterranean areas like Languedoc, ordinary agricultural workers might drink more than a litre of wine a day and not come to any harm. In the sixteenth century wine was a pleasure, and a soft drug: the Latins were wise enough not to become drunkards. This was not true of certain zones where drinking was excessive – in the western provinces of France, for example, or Germany, not to mention other countries further north. Wine was in fact a source of calories. They may have been poor quality calories, but they did at least help the peasants to keep warm and to work.

Finally, wine was pure and healthy by the standards of the time: the alcohol it contained killed most of the germs. It was safer to drink wine than dangerous, polluted water which often came from infected sources in the towns and countryside. Wine, at this period, meant health. A poor wine harvest was a real misfortune; wine-growing was therefore an important part of agriculture. It should be added that the wine of the period did not contain any chemical additives which today, rightly or wrongly, come in for a lot of criticism.

The sixteenth century

It is true that some vineyards in the far north were abandoned during the sixteenth century as a result of regional specialization, which was already beginning to develop, based on variation in the local soils and climate. Competition from southern wines, which had the advantage of a sunnier climate, was also a factor in the retreat of the vine. This process had begun in England in the fourteenth century as a result of various factors, including competition from Bordeaux wines and, perhaps, a slight cooling of the climate. The few remaining vineyards were now abandoned there and in Flanders; in the *bocages* (hedge-enclosed fields) of western France and in Normandy too, marginal vineyards were destroyed. In Normandy there was a switch to cider production, which developed throughout the sixteenth century and which provided the same benefits as wine in the diet.[18]

These were extreme cases. On the whole, the vineyards of the north, when they were not too far north, were expanding, in terms of the amount of land under cultivation, during the prosperous periods of the sixteenth century until about 1560. In Hurepoix and the area south of Paris, where wine-growing is almost non-existent today, 5 to 7% of the land under cultivation (which in these fertile regions meant virtually all the land available) was given over to vines in 1550.[19] The urban market stimulated production (there were at least 100,000 wine consumers in the city around 1500), and the vines themselves were rejuvenated by the introduction of strains from the south of France. Between 1540 and 1560 wine production was still expanding.

Certain regions, for example eastern Languedoc, which already had a lot of vines, did not increase them much during the sixteenth century. Vines in these areas accounted for 12 to 15% of the land under cultivation around 1550. Elsewhere the villagers planted a great many vines during the Renaissance, encouraged by the Atlantic trade and by the possibility of transporting wine by river on the

Loire, the Garonne and the Seine. With this valuable product to sell, they became involved with the market; they earned some money; and obtained maximum returns from the stony land which is suitable for the vine but gives low cereal yields. I refer in particular to the slopes and hillsides which are more likely to produce quality wines than any kind of cereal. Thus it was possible to break through the Malthusian ceilings, thanks to an increase in productivity, not in terms of a higher yield per hectare, but in terms of a higher value as a result of concentrating on crops suitable for each particular region.

On the Atlantic coast, cultivation of the vine continued to increase during the Renaissance, thanks to demand from England and especially from the Netherlands. In Nantes wine exports had dropped from 12,000 hectolitres a year in 1355 to 2,700 hectolitres a year round 1446–8. During the sixteenth century, however, these exports rose to 99,000 hectolitres a year in 1555 and had even exceptionally reached 300,000 hectolitres by 1572!

The situation in Bordeaux was not so good. The high levels of production which had been reached before the Black Death were not reached again – the Malthusian ceilings we have already discussed were operating. At the beginning of the fourteenth century the enormous quantity of 850,000 hectolitres of wine a year was exported from the port of Bordeaux, mostly to England. Then came the great crisis of the early Middle Ages. Finally during the years 1530 to 1560, despite a partial recovery, the record levels of the period before the Black Death were only rarely equalled. The normal levels of 1530–60 were distinctly lower. Only 225,000 hectolitres of wine were exported from Bordeaux under Henri II (approximate annual average). It was not possible, in this case, even to restore completely the levels of the brilliant but distant past.

Gardens and market gardens were also important, for the peasantry as well as the townspeople. We should not exaggerate their contribution, however. In the area around

Nîmes gardens, with or without irrigation, were an established tradition. However, around 1550 they only accounted for a small part (in terms of value) of the agricultural land. In 179 villages, gardens accounted for only 2% of the overall value of the 179 corresponding territories. It should be pointed out, however, that in the west of France production of hemp, often cultivated in gardens, had already led to the development of a significant linen industry (linen which was used for clothes and sails).

What was the position of stockbreeding between 1500 and 1600? This was, of course, strongly oriented towards the market; but at this period livestock prices were falling relative to those of non-animal products. In Paris between 1510 and 1540–80 wheat prices rose faster and more steeply than prices for eggs, sheep and probably also for cattle. This came about because the vast majority of consumers concentrated their spending power on grain and bread, which was their staple diet. There was little money left over to spend on animal protein. Only the wealthier consumers could afford meat in any significant quantity. This led to the notorious vicious circle of traditional agriculture: the farmers largely produced grain and other 'vegetable' crops. They neglected cattle, sheep and fertilizers. As a result of this lack of fertilizer, yields were low, so that more land had to be given over to grain and other crops, with the result that there was even less land left over for livestock and so on... In those 179 villages in the diocese of Nîmes around 1550, for example, only 13% of the land, in terms of value, was given over to the rearing of cattle, sheep and pigs, whereas 63% was devoted to cereal crops and chestnuts (which were also rich in carbohydrates); 15.7% of the land, in terms of value, was used for vines. In Languedoc between 1520 and 1530 stockbreeding suffered disastrous crises as a result of epidemics. The number of animals was severely reduced and these losses were not to be made good for the next eighty years because the economic climate did not favour livestock.

If we look now at Spain, we do not, at present, have access to many series of tithes, at least for the fifteenth century, and a few which would be relevant for the sixteenth century have not yet been studied in depth (in particular in Majorca).[20] In order to establish the trend in agricultural production we therefore have to rely on other data.

According to Gonzalo Anes, the growth of towns during the sixteenth century meant that agricultural production remained stable, and in certain cases, increased. On the other hand, the importance of external demand for Spanish agricultural products has been exaggerated: I refer in particular to the hypothetical demand from the new Spanish colonies of the New World. This demand was not strong enough to have had any serious influence on agricultural production, except in a few regions near the coast (like the Basque country) which had modernized and diversified.[21] The factors which were really responsible for the development of agriculture in Spain during the sixteenth century had more to do with the growth in population and with a change of attitude on the part of the landlords who, from this time on, wanted their estates to be settled and cultivated.[22]

Whatever the reasons, the area of land under cultivation in the huge peninsula gradually increased from the end of the fifteenth century, especially in the two Castilles and in Andalusia.

In New Castille the expansion of arable farming was limited by the need for stockraising to survive. The peasants needed oxen both to pull their ploughs and to provide manure for the fields, even if the quantities were minute, so they required much pasture which could not be converted into cereal fields.

There is also evidence of some local specialization in cereal crops, vines and olives, especially in New Castille. On the whole, in Spain, as elsewhere in the sixteenth century, an increase in population led to the taking into cultivation of poor and marginal land. However, the soil in areas which had been newly cleared, or cleared again, was not good, and yields tended to decline fairly rapidly. Increased demand thus caused the price of wheat to rise, especially in Andalusia, Castille and Valencia. On the other hand, the increase in wine prices in the first half of the sixteenth century stimulated the planting of vines: it also encouraged a partial shift from cereals to vines.

Permanent grazing land became scarce in Spain during the sixteenth century as a result of the expansion of arable farming. Plough-teams were affected: the oxen badly needed this pasture land. They began to be replaced by mules which could be fed on oats and barley, two crops produced in the very fields which had just been taken into cultivation. This increase in the number of mules is also to be found in France in the sixteenth century and more generally throughout the *ancien régime*.

In Spain the increase in production, especially of cereal crops, made it possible to support a larger population. In this context the increases in tithes and ground rents should not be seen as entirely parasitic. Adam Smith reminds us that the volume of the stomachs of the rich is not very different from that of the poor. The clergy and landowners in Spain did not consume all the grain they took from the peasants: a part was resold in the towns and the countryside; or they gave it to their servants – in other words, it helped to feed a fair number of people in town and country. The tithe paid to the Church might have been regarded as parasitic in the country, but not in the towns which obtained at least part of their food from this source. Anes' comments on Spain can also be applied, incidentally, to the Paris region in 1580–90: the popular enthusiasm for the Catholic League can be explained in part by the fact that in the capital the Church was seen not as a predator but as a source of supply. It distributed the grain it levied from the farms in the Paris Basin to the urban population, sometimes, but not always, making a charge.

After this general outline, which owes much to Gonzalo

Anes, I shall deal briefly with the various Spanish regions. For this I shall draw again on the work of Anes, and also on the contributions to the 1977 conference. In Old Castille, in the province of Segovia, the 'ceilings' of the sixteenth century were the logical consequence of economic and demographic expansion. This expansion had begun during the second half of the fifteenth century and continued steadily until it reached a peak in the third quarter of the sixteenth century. If ones takes the period 1600–49 as representing a base-line of 100, the two decades between 1570 and 1590 reached a level of 136 (134 and 138 respectively) before the great decline of the period 1590 to 1660. This prosperity of the 1570s and the 1580s was based on the production of wheat for consumption in towns. In this way the towns supported the favourable trend of the sixteenth century.

In the province of Murcia, Lemeunier too points out the high level of grain production in the middle years of the sixteenth century (1557–61). The last quarter of this century (1579–1603) was still within the period of high cereal production. The real crisis only began in 1604.

In the maritime Basque country there was an undeniable period of growth between the ecclesiastical survey of 1537–42 and that of 1588–92.[23] This expansion continued until at least 1580. It was significant in the coastal regions where it was stimulated by trade and industry, and also in the valley of the Ebro, where the wine-producing areas responded to the expansion of trade. Cereal production increased by 70% and wine production by 65% between the two dates mentioned above. (In the wine-growing region of the Ebro agriculture was to concentrate exclusively on vines during the eighteenth century.) On the other hand, in the area between these two regions, a hilly area between 400 and 800 metres high, the expansion was distinctly less impressive: the production of cereals and of leguminous crops like beans increased by only 29% between these two dates.

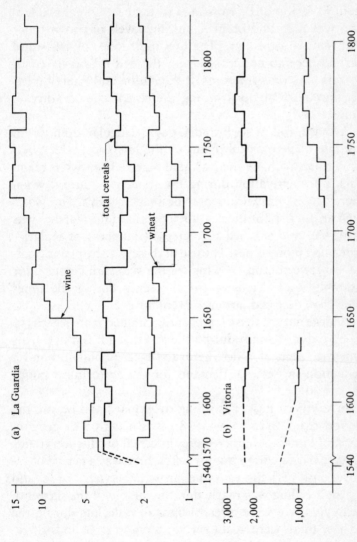

6. Development of the gross agribultural product in the Spanish Basque country, 1537–1850 (Bilbao and de Pinedo)

The work of the Italians Anata, Landi and Basini, as well as that of Aymard, gives us a general idea of the situation in the second half of the sixteenth century in northern Italy, from Emilia and the Romagna to Liguria. Cereal production was high and often rising; the levels of productivity and returns were high. The first indications of crisis and decline became noticeable from the end of the sixteenth century, but the symptoms of stagnation and even of crisis became more obvious during the seventeenth century in Italy.

Aymard, following Braudel, pays particular attention to the fate of the coastal plains or the lowlands, which had been almost abandoned around 1450. They were taken back into cultivation during the sixteenth century, when there was major investment in drainage systems. This was a high health risk for the peasants: the silt of the marshes was disturbed and this led to increased numbers of malaria-spreading mosquitoes. The use of these marshy plains oscillated between crop-growing (in the sixteenth century, for example) and extensive stockbreeding during the times they were deserted (around 1450, for example).

A large part of these temporarily drained marshes was to be abandoned again during the seventeenth century. This was the result of a decline in the local population and a reduction in external demand for the agricultural goods they produced.

In southern Italy, according to Aymard and Basini, the period from 1450 to 1560–80 was a period of growth. Certain familiar characteristics in cereal production trends emerge particularly strongly here: there was a period of recovery or perhaps of rapid growth between 1460 and 1530; a ceiling was reached in the middle of the sixteenth century; there were already signs of a decline during the 1590s; there were again certain temporary periods of recovery during the seventeenth century; and the modest expansion in the eighteenth century came to an end around 1750–60.

When Aymard discusses southern Italy he gives particular attention to the case of Sicily. According to him, cereal production in Sicily between 1450 and 1560–80 kept pace with the increase in population (which rose by between 50 and 100% in different parts of the island). Nonetheless, it became more and more of a struggle in Sicily and in the rest of southern Italy after 1520–30 to satisfy the demand for grain, whether this demand was local or foreign, or came from the army or the towns. This was one of the reasons for the rise in prices. We should add that export licences (or *tratte*) were often refused, and in any case were heavily taxed. One sees the same problem in Languedoc: there the provincial Estates refused more and more export licences for cereals during the first half of the sixteenth century; it had been much more liberal in the last half of the fifteenth century. In any case, to return to Sicily, grain exports slowed down from 1510 to 1520. From 1550 to 1590 'they remained stable and their share in the total production of the island tended to decline'.[24] There was thus a relative increase in consumption of grain on the island itself, at the expense of exports.

There was at the same time an increase in land prices in Sicily; rents and certain important seigneurial dues (not unlike the French *champarts* or *terrages*) also increased. Demographic expansion meant that less land was available: this led to conflicts between the great landowners and the rural communities over ownership and the use of the land, especially when huge areas of uncultivated land were involved. The price of grazing land increased, perhaps because it had become rarer as a result of land clearance. This meant that the great landowners tended to restrict the sale of their estates, which they consolidated by means of entails in order to prevent them from being broken up.

There were other crops in Sicily such as sugar, silk and wine, which were grown primarily for the market. These showed the same tendency towards expansion, as did

Apulian wool. In a few specialized regions silk represented half the value of grain production around 1600. It even approached wheat, as far as the overall value of exports was concerned. However, wheat prices increased twice as fast as silk prices during this period: the lack of good land had a more harmful effect on the supply of grain than on that of silk (the silk worm does not need a large area of ground to multiply, and mulberry bushes can be grown on the poor soil of the hillsides). The smaller increase in silk prices was also responsible for the fact that silk became available to a wider section of the population.

This cycle of expansion in Sicily came to an end during the 1590s, but this was not simply the result of the bad harvests of this decade, which Braudel rightly emphasizes. In fact, this series of poor harvests in Sicily coincided with a lasting reduction in the amount of land given over to cereals: 'this reduction was the outcome of a serious economic and social crisis which had begun fifteen years earlier'.[25] But in Sicily, unlike the France of Catherine de Medici, there had not been any wars of religion which might explain this crisis.

The slackening of economic growth which occurred in Sicily in the 1590s was linked to the underlying demographic stabilization. One reason for this was that plague was rife on the island between 1576 and 1585. In this context, the urban and rural revolts in the kingdom of Naples around 1585 appear to be significant.[26] Have they any connection with the disturbed state of rural life and with the decrease in agricultural production? In Sicily around 1590 there were characteristics reminiscent of Normandy in the 1430s, though in Normandy they were more severe. At the end of the sixteenth century peasants in Sicily had a heavy debt to shoulder. The middle class of the agricultural world – the yeomen, known locally as *massari* – was partially ruined. There is even evidence of 'strike' action on the part of candidates for leases (as there was later in Languedoc, around 1690); they refused to lease land from the landowners: the rent demanded appeared to them excessive.

What is more, the towns were tending to take a bigger slice of the cake, in terms of both public and private spending. Municipal revenue was raised through income tax, through *tratte* or export duties levied on grain, through money lending and through rents.[27] (A similar situation arose in Perigord at about the same time: in 1593 local rebels, or *croquants,* rose up against the towns of the area which they accused of fleecing them.) In Sicily and in southern Italy the State, the great landowners and the merchants tended to appropriate all the profits which could give rise to a market-oriented agriculture: 'they left the peasant producer nothing but the risks'.

These were the reasons why the great cycle of agricultural expansion came to an end in the late sixteenth century in southern Italy and in Sicily, as in other parts of Europe at about this time. Once again, as far as the sixteenth century is concerned, the tithe series do not reveal anything particularly unexpected. They show a remarkable uniformity: high ceilings of production were reached everywhere. We shall not find such a consistent pattern when we look at the next period of expansion, in the eighteenth century.

I shall now conclude this chapter on the sixteenth century, or, more especially, on the agricultural 'renaissance': different countries experienced this at different times but the period in question stretches, roughly, from 1460 to 1560–1600. I shall now try to place the figures for tithe and agricultural productivity in a more general context. I can make the following points:

(1) Agricultural production generally increased during the sixteenth century. But in the cases for which we have information about production and population for the fourteenth century, this increase often appears as no more than the recovery of the old levels (and not even complete at that); these levels had already been reached in the first third or the first half of the fourteenth century before the Black

Death. It is obvious that all this is true only for certain regions of Western Europe; Central and Eastern Europe followed a different pattern.

(2) This increase or recovery of agricultural production during the Renaissance and the sixteenth century was equalled (and often surpassed) by increases in population: in other words, productivity and share per capita tended to diminish. From the global point of view the sixteenth century was a period of prosperity, but from the point of view of per capita revenue or consumption it was a harsh period.

(3) This pauperization at the individual level took two forms:

(a) real wages tended to fall;

(b) farms or holdings tended to be divided into smaller and smaller units which often became scarcely viable. The rise in population took place in an agricultural context in which there was only a limited amount of good land available. The remaining forests had to be preserved to satisfy the need for firewood, hunting, building and so on. In France in particular it can be shown that the lack of land available for taking into cultivation was due to the survival of enormous forests, which declined only with the last phases of development in the seventeenth and, above all, the eighteenth centuries.[28]

(4) Prices, and in particular grain prices, rose for two reasons. In the first place, the cost of grain production on marginal, not very fertile land was increasing. In the second place, demand for grain was increasing relative to supply. Rent also increased, but at different rates in different regions – more slowly in the south, for example, than in the north. This unequal but undeniable increase in the rent for land was due to the fact that there was more and more competition for leases. The leaseholders were often quite rich and they wanted at any price to obtain from the landowners the right to lease their lands.

(5) The increase of the gross product in the sixteenth

century could not go on for ever, even if it was sometimes a pure and simple recovery of the pre-1348 levels. On some occasions there was a slowing down. In France, for example, this was already noticeable after 1500 compared with the more rapid growth of the previous four decades. In Sicily there was a similar slowing down of growth *circa* 1520–50. In general, the increase in agricultural productivity which I have been describing as typical of the 'sixteenth century' came to an end towards 1560–70, or at various dates between 1570 and 1600.

(6) Some regions were privileged: the Netherlands, the environs of great cities like Paris, and regions which were near the sea or had other transport facilities. Whether or not the increase in cereal production was, from the quantitative point of view, no more than a return to pre-1348 levels, it was always accompanied by new *qualitative* changes based on the diversification of production into stockbreeding, viticulture, the production of vegetables, hemp, linen etc. In these areas such qualitative changes were for long-term growth more important than the simple quantitative recovery of the pre-1348 levels of output which I have been stressing. In any case the increase in stockbreeding is more obvious in the Netherlands in the sixteenth century than in Languedoc, where it is even possible to speak of a decline of stockbreeding as a result of the spread of arable farming in general, and cereal production in particular.

In the next chapter I shall examine what has long been called the 'seventeenth-century crisis' – a crisis which is better seen as a phenomenon of stabilization, stagnation or normalization.

7

The seventeenth century: general crisis or stabilization?

On the whole, despite many fluctuations, the product of the tithe became more stable during the seventeenth century. We can, if we like, talk of a general crisis in the seventeenth century, but the situation, at least in France, was not the same as that produced by the dramatic collapses of the fourteenth and fifteenth centuries. In the seventeenth century cereal production did not necessarily fall *permanently* below the ceilings reached in the sixteenth century (or, shall we say, below the levels of recovery equal to those which had been reached before the Black Death of 1348). But it often fluctuated around levels distinctly lower than these 'ceilings', at least during a few particularly dangerous periods. In any case, cereal production, at least in France, did not often exceed the levels mentioned above. It would be more accurate to talk of a period of stagnation or stability (stabilization or 'normalization') rather than of 'general crisis' in the seventeenth century.

As far as the medium, as opposed to the long, term is concerned, one thing is clear: whatever the differences in timing between one European country and another, there was a general crisis in Europe around 1640–50 – the result of wars, taxes, the weather, occasional revolutions and possibly a shortage of precious metals for minting.[1]

I shall begin my general study of the seventeenth century by looking at certain regions of Central Europe for which, it must be said, the term 'stagnation' is not strong enough: the situation there in the seventeenth century was like that in France at the end of the Middle Ages – a state of economic decline.

According to Lászlo Makkai, there was a steady decline in the grain tithe in Hungary from the 1570s to about 1590–1600. This decline levelled off for several decades around the middle or the second third of the seventeenth century. Then came a further decline, especially after 1670; and finally a period of recovery after 1710. Between 1570 and 1710 grain production – in so far as this can be measured from the tithe – declined by about 50%.[2]

One of the main causes of this decline was war – for example the 'fifteen years' war' in Hungary from 1591 to 1606. After 1671 there was a series of civil wars, which were followed by a difficult period of campaigns against the Turks in 1683 to 1699. Finally there was the Hungarian War of Independence against the Hapsburgs (1703–11). As in Western Europe, and perhaps to an even greater extent, these various wars brought with them other epidemics, famines and so on.

War was an important factor, but it should not lead us back to 'drum and trumpet history'. Makkai demonstrates that there were negative factors which had nothing to do with war, and which help to account for the decline in the tithe in Hungary. Around the town of Sopron in western Hungary, for example, this decline began around 1570, well before the fifteen years' war (1591–1606). It continued until 1620: so it carried on into the fifteen years of peace which followed this war. In this case the recession was essentially an economic one, not directly linked with any war.

The decline in agriculture in Hungary in the seventeenth century was no doubt accompanied by a fall in population, although Hungarian historians have not paid much attention to this particular point. They have stressed some factors which link seventeenth-century Hungary with certain important, but not irreversible, changes that had occurred in Western Europe in the fourteenth and fifteenth centuries. It seems that a characteristic of the first phase of the depression in Hungary between 1570 to 1620 was the abandoning of marginal lands, which had unwisely been taken into cultivation during the period of expansion before 1570. In the less prosperous seventeenth century wheat was on the whole grown only on the most fertile land; this practice led to an increase in the productivity of the land per hectare: the sheaves of wheat thus became heavier. Instead of yielding an average of 3 litres of grain, as had been the case during the last forty years of the sixteenth century, the average sheaf of wheat yielded 5 litres of grain in the 1680s and 1690s. On the other hand, the fact that the marginal lands were no longer used for cereals helped to stimulate wine-growing, and, still more, stock-breeding, which was to flourish on these abandoned lands. Meat consumption increased in Hungary in the seventeenth century, just as it had done in the countries of Western Europe in the fourteenth and fifteenth centuries at a time when fields which had previously been used for grain could easily be converted back to pasture and when, on the other hand, the very high real wages paid to a reduced working population meant that they could well afford to buy meat. During the seventeenth century the average adult Hungarian's intake of food was 3,500 calories a day; their diet now contained an increasingly large proportion of protein and wine, and less cereal. The percentage of secondary cereal, like oats and barley, which were grown as animal foodstuffs, also tended to rise (a rise which is reflected in the percentages of different cereals in the tithe). This is yet another indication of the growing importance of livestock.

In Poland, just as in Hungary, the peak of cereal production had been reached around 1570.[3] After this there was a levelling off and even a slight decline in cereal production between 1570 and 1650, amounting to a decrease in production of about 10% in relation to the ceiling of 1570. Exports of grain from Poland to the Netherlands remained important, however. We should remember that

The seventeenth century

Polish agriculture was divided into two basic sectors: there were the manors or great estates; and the small farms of peasant families producing to feed themselves. It was essentially the peasant sector that was declining, a decline which can be explained in part by the increase in forced labour. The peasants, who had been enserfed, had to carry out these *corvées* on the great seigneurial estates – they made the manors richer ... and the peasants poorer.

After 1650 the decline in cereal production in Poland was no longer insidious – it had become dramatic, but in fact it is not difficult to explain this. The drop was sometimes as high as 50 to 60% of the gross product; it was connected with the great Northern War of the 1650s. This was followed by a period of recovery until about 1690, when production was about 70% of the 1570 level. It was thus only a partial recovery, for the following reasons: for a long period grain prices were low, there was a lack of capital in Poland itself, demand – both internal and external – was low, and finally Poland also suffered from competition from other exporting countries (from the 1660s English grain exports increased at the expense of those from the Baltic countries). Further wars broke out in Poland around 1700 to 1715 and production fell back to about 50% of the ceiling levels of the 1570s. The final long period of recovery began properly during the second third of the eighteenth century.

These damaging, then frankly disastrous, events in seventeenth-century Poland were not in principle unlike those in France and Germany at the same period. However, the drop in population and in production was much more catastrophic in Poland than in France. It was more on the scale of the disasters which had shaken Germany a little earlier, during the Thirty Years' War.

Let us now look at France. We can then compare the situation there with that in neighbouring countries in Western Europe, especially in the Netherlands.

It should be made clear from the start that France was

experiencing a very long period of stabilization which contained within itself three extensive and successive periods of depression. This period of fluctuating stabilization lasted, as a matter of fact, from 1560 to 1715. It is what French historians call the 'long seventeenth century' – long indeed, since it lasted 155 years! It is, of course, possible to link this long-term depression with a certain lack of precious metals, itself the result of insufficient production from the American silver mines. This is the traditional explanation, somewhat outdated now, which accounts for the crisis in terms of monetary factors. According to Morineau this explanation is at best inadequate.

In fact in the very long term the period of stabilization in France in the seventeenth century was marked by certain typical characteristics, as far as demographic patterns and cereal production were concerned: these characteristics are also to be found before the Black Death and again during the period of vigorous recovery around 1550–60. They included a population of around 19 million inhabitants or more, cereal yields which had hardly increased in relation to the high ceilings of the later Middle Ages, and grain harvests which, when they can be measured in the seventeenth century, are not much higher than they had been during the first third of the fourteenth century. This is why, in spite of the enormous fluctuations between 1340 and 1560, I could speak of a very long phase of 'immobile history' (1320–1720), at the end of which the old ecosystem was more or less reproduced, even though some increase was recorded in between.[4]

However, we are historians not ecologists; chronology is all important. It is immediately obvious that the two dates I mentioned as the limits of the long seventeenth century in France – *viz.* 1560 and 1715 – have significant political and military connotations. 1560 marks the beginning of the Wars of Religion. These were to inflict terrible damage on the French economy and reduce the population. 1715 marks the death of Louis XIV. This occurred immediately after a financially disastrous war which had devastated a large part of France (even if it brought prosperity to a few coastal areas like Marseilles, or Saint-Malo).[5] The War of the Spanish Succession, crowned, if I may use that expression, by the death of Louis XIV, was followed by several decades of peace; these proved a useful stimulus for the French economy, which recovered and even expanded. This expansion, however, was also the result of other factors unconnected with national or international politics.

I have pointed out that the long-term stabilization of French agriculture – at least as far as cereals were concerned – during the long seventeenth century (from 1560 to 1715) was disturbed by three major periods of depression. The first period coincided with the Wars of Religion, approximately 1560–95. The second also occurred during a time of war – the Thirty Years' War and the Fronde, during the 1630s, the 1640s and the early 1650s; agriculture in the different regions was affected at different times within this period. The third period of depression occurred during the crisis at the end of Louis XIV's reign, which was in fact a very long 'end of reign', marked by bloody and especially costly wars between 1690 and 1713.

Let us now look at the figures for the decline in the tithe during the Wars of Religion in an area stretching from Cambrai and Namur to Paris, Dijon, Clermont-Ferrand, Montpellier and Arles. In the northern regions (I mean north of Paris), the 10% tithe was about a third lower between 1580 and 1600 compared with the high levels or ceilings that had been reached during the period 1540–60 before the Wars of Religion; in the Paris region the tithe product declined by about a fifth or a quarter. In the east, the centre and the south of France, that is to say, in Burgundy, the Auvergne, the Mediterranean and the area around Lyons, it declined by about 39%; it was 32.7% in Normandy.[6] These decreases were severe everywhere, especially in the south, which suffered a great deal from religious wars – some of which were directed against the

Protestant movements which were very active in the south.

It is possible that the curves for the tithe product were artificially depressed as a result of strikes on the part of the tithe payers who were influenced by Huguenot propaganda. There is, however, no doubt that the depression in these curves *also* reflects a reduction in the real agricultural product, especially during the worst period of religious wars, after 1585. In fact, income or levies such as rents which were not affected by strikes also declined during the same period. The common factor linking the decline in the tithe with the decline of rents is thus to be found in the fall in the gross agricultural product itself. This fall affected cereals and also products such as woad, wines from Charentes after 1572 etc. In real terms, this depression lasted on and off for thirty years – it was perhaps the price to be paid for the introduction of Protestantism which imposed religious, political and social changes on rural society. This intrusion from outside certainly had a profound effect on the rural ecosystem after 1560. Religious reforms, however justifiable in other ways, had the effect of disturbing this relatively stable system which I have described by the expression 'immobile history'. This disturbance provoked strong reactions, and was, unfortunately, to lead a century later, to the Revocation of the Edict of Nantes (1685). But that is another story...

The decline in the gross agricultural product between 1560 and 1595 helps us to understand certain phenomena. It is clear that subsistence crises were more likely to occur, and did indeed occur more frequently during this period: in years which suffered bad weather the average level of cereal production during the period of religious wars was consistently lower than the 'normal' level.

In fact these subsistence crises were both severe and recurrent between 1560 and 1575, and again between 1584 and 1595. Between 1580 and 1595 there were also numerous peasant revolts, often against taxes, in Dauphiny, Normandy, Brittany, Perigord, Velay etc.: the rebels

were provoked to action by the decline in the gross agricultural product which made the royal taxes (which remained
the same, or even increased) an impossible burden for
them. What is more, the population declined during the
Wars of Religion, though these losses were not so severe as
those which occurred in the fourteenth and fifteenth centuries.

The French population may have declined by a few
million during the Wars of Religion, although it is difficult
to estimate accurately; all the same, these figures do not
approach the 10 million lost around 1450, at least if one
compares the low population figures for that time with the
demographic peak which had been reached around 1328.
As far as the decline in cereal production is concerned, it
was not so severe during the Wars of Religion as during the
Hundred Years' War. In the last third of the sixteenth
century grain production declined by about 33% relative
to the levels of the pre-war period, whereas around 1430–
40 the decrease had been probably more, in relation to the
highly productive period before the Black Death.[7]

Germany, and in particular Alsace – which was not, of
course, yet part of France – was spared religious wars. In
Alsace the tithe product declined by only 7.3% between the
good period (1548–83) and the less good period (1584–
95). During this rather troubled decade the west bank of
the Rhine was disturbed by brigands and soldiers from the
neighbouring areas of France, unsettled by the Wars of Religion. The modest extent of the crisis in Alsace emphasizes,
by contrast, the devastating effects of the Wars of Religion
in France. Whether or not there was a state of war is clearly
an important factor in economic history, at least on the
Continent, which was sometimes 'isolated' in this respect.

If Alsace (and Germany) was spared, the Netherlands,
on the other hand, suffered badly from what we may refer
to as the European wars of religion. This time it was not
only the French involved: Huguenots against Papists. It
was a struggle between Catholic Spain and the Protestant

Netherlands. As Van der Wee has pointed out, the revolt of the Netherlands against Spain began in 1568 (as opposed to 1560 for the outbreak of relgious conflict in France).[8] 'This war in the Netherlands, especially after the 1570s, involved large-scale military campaigns and caused enormous distress. In nearly all areas it had a severely damaging effect on agriculture. The armies lived off the countryside for years, and they constantly plundered villages and hamlets.' According to the Belgian historian, the most severe damage began in the north (in Zealand and Holland, or, in other words, in the area known as the Netherlands today) between 1573 and 1575. The devastation then spread towards the south (into present-day Belgium) after the sack of Antwerp in 1576. 'In Brabant', writes Van der Wee, 'rents and income from the tithe had already dropped by 1576–1577, whereas in Namur, Flanders, Hainault and Limburg this occurred in 1577–1578.' Incidentally, in various regions in France, especially in Dauphiny and in Languedoc, the year 1577 also represented one of the lowest points in the curve of tithes, in kind or calculated in real terms. In connection with the devastation of Wallonia, Van der Wee remarks that 'even the neutral area governed by the Prince-Bishop of Liège did not escape damage from the movement of troops and garrisons, and this led to a drop in agricultural revenue'.

I have tried elsewhere to estimate how far the income from the tithe and from rents declined as a result of the wars in the Netherlands during the last third or the last quarter of the sixteenth century, in the most important areas around Antwerp, Liège, Namur and Cambrai.[9] If one compares the period 1570–1600 with the more peaceful, earlier period (1550–70), one may conclude that the tithe (expressed in real terms) and rents declined by about a third between these two dates. In the shorter term, between the high levels of 1570 and the lower ones of 1580–5, there was an even sharper decline of about 50% in the tithe and rents. In this situation the probability of subsistence crises was higher than normal in the Netherlands, and they did in fact occur.

Van der Wee does not give precise figures for this; he thinks that 'the decline in the gross product in the last quarter of the sixteenth century, especially in the Southern Netherlands (now Belgium) was enormous'.[10] He explains this drop 'in production and productivity' by the fact that 'a lot of farms were burnt, the fields remained unploughed for years as a result of the death or flight of the owners or the tenants'. However, 'elsewhere the pillage did not last so long, and the farmers who had fled returned home quite quickly'.

After the depression associated with the religious wars in France and in the Netherlands there was once again, between 1600 and 1640, a long period of recovery in France, as far as cereal production was concerned. In the Paris region the capital reached a level of 400,000 inhabitants for the first time in 1637, and 500,000 around 1680.[11] In these conditions the period of recovery developed into a period of real growth; during the 1640s cereal production around Paris substantially exceeded the previous records of around 1580.[12] Desaive and Constant have pointed out that investment in real estate proved very profitable around Paris for the landowners in the first half of the seventeenth century. Returns on capital invested in land could reach 15 to 17%; this was the result not only of increased grain production, but also of the fact that the landowners were squeezing the farmers more outrageously than they had done in the earlier period.

In Alsace, too (as in the Netherlands), yields of tithes in the first third of the seventeenth century were better ($+12\%$) than they had been during the good period in the sixteenth century (1500 to 1583). In Savoy, the recent work of Jean Nicolas indicates a high level of cereal production around 1620 (according to the tithe figures of Menthon).

Let us leave the Paris region, Alsace and Savoy. Elsewhere, the recovery of cereal production under Louis XIII bears comparison with the good periods of the sixteenth century; there was sometimes a complete recovery, for example in the case of Normandy and the area around Lyons.[13] The recent work of Garnier on Normandy confirms that there was a high ceiling in cereal production in 1600–40. This ceiling equalled or even exceeded the best local levels of the sixteenth century, which had been achieved under Henri II and Charles IX, between 1550 and 1560. In other areas, for example Burgundy, the Auvergne and the Mediterranean, the levels achieved under Louis XIII remained lower than the previous records of the sixteenth century. If one sets aside the dynamic Paris region, then during the first years of Richelieu's ministry, around 1625, the tithe product equalled but hardly ever surpassed the levels recorded under Henri II and Charles IX, between 1550 and 1560.

Around 1640–50, sometimes from the 1630s on, or from the beginning of the 1650s, we have evidence of a new and serious period of depression in France, especially in the north. This took place at much the same time as similar recessions in other parts of Europe, and perhaps even in England during the revolutions of the 1640s. For the moment, though, let us remain in France: what we may call the accident of the Thirty Years' War and the Fronde had a different effect in the various regions.

(a) In the north-east, in the Cambrésis, Alsace etc. it was a large-scale disaster lasting for just over twenty years from 1632. The tithe product, and probably also the gross product in real terms, was slashed by 50%.

(b) In the Paris region this bad period was rather less catastrophic: in the years around 1650 rents declined in real terms by between 10 and 20%.

(c) In the central provinces there was also a short but distinct recession.

(d) Finally, the south of France was not affected.

The years 1660–80, or more precisely 1663–85, are interesting. Historians working on the 'Colbert' period (as far as I am concerned 'Colbert' is simply a form of short-hand, rather as one might refer to 'the Victorian period' – I am not concerned with the personality cult of the minister) have for a long time defined it as a 'period of crisis'. It is true that wheat prices during Colbert's ministry in the 1660s, 1670s and the 1680s were very low (at least after the brief inflation caused by and during the famine of 1661). In Simiand's terms, this was a 'phase B' of low prices.[14] But could we not look at this the other way round? If prices were low, this was also because wheat harvests were good, over and above the post-Fronde recovery. It was thus not a question, after 1663, of a crisis which would curtail production, even if the farmers sometimes had trouble selling their grain at a profit. In fact, once the famine of 1661 (which particularly affected the Paris Basin) was over, the following two decades, that is to say the 1660s, the 1670s and to some extent the 1680s, were marked by high levels of cereal production in Languedoc, Provence, the Bordelais, Perigord, Auvergne and Upper Normandy. Elsewhere there was a post-Fronde or post-Thirty Years' War recovery: this is evident in the Ile-de-France, in Picardy, the Cambrésis, Alsace and Burgundy. Recent research (later than our book of 1972) on Maine-Anjou and Lower Normandy (Garnier and Pavard), on the Beauce (Constant), on Poitou (Péret), on Brittany (Tim le Goff, see Figure 13), on Savoy (Jean Nicolas) and on the southern domains of the Knights of St John (Gangneux) fully support this time scale.[15] There was thus a period of relatively high grain production during the 1660s, 1670s, and even 1680s. It is true that the record levels of the six-teenth century were rarely exceeded, except perhaps in the Mediterranean region of France. But the relative abun-dance of the Colbert years put an end to famine for nearly thirty years, from 1663 to 1691. This coincided with the better years of the Sun King – the period of Racine, Molière and Colbert. (No correlations with the great writers, of course!) This plentiful supply of grain was connected with the stability or low level of grain prices at this time. In these circumstances it was fairly easy to feed the soldiers of the French army and the workers on the great building sites (at Versailles or on the construction of the Canal du Midi); it was also possible to feed the workers in the few new factories established at Colbert's instigation. Later on, a priest from the south was to call these relatively prosperous years 'the time of the fat ears of grain'.

After 1680, and especially after 1690, a new period of depression set in: it was connected with the wars of the second phase of Louis XIV's reign, and with the high tax levels of the period. This depression is evident in Languedoc, Provence, the Bordelais, Perigord, Aquitaine, the Lyons region, the Auvergne, the Cambrésis. It is also evident in the Ile-de-France, but only after 1700: Paris, a formidable centre of growth resistant to the crisis, seems to have created a relatively or temporarily protected sector around herself.

Recent research (since 1971–2) has also found evidence of an 'end-of-reign crisis' for Louis XIV in Normandy (Garnier), but not in the rich plain around Caen (Garnier and Pavard, see Figure 11); in the Beauce (Constant), in Poitou (Péret's study on the Duchy of Meilleraie), in Savoy, according to Jean Nicolas (the tithe declined here by 22.6% between 1680–5 and 1700–5). Finally, in the southern French domains of the Knights of St John, the tithe fell by 32.2% in real terms between the 1670s and 1710–20, according to Gangneux (see Figure 12).

In Brittany, however, there was no real depression at the end of Louis XIV's reign, more a period of stabilization. If one takes the tithe product in the decade 1640–50 as a base of 100, in 1660–88 this rose to 117, and it levelled out at 117.6 in 1690–1715. We should remember that during this period at the end of the seventeenth century and the beginning of the eighteenth century Britanny enjoyed a certain relative prosperity, or at least an immunity against depression. This was particularly clear in the case of the 'boom' of the port of Saint-Malo at this period. Alsace and Burgundy also seem to have been more or less protected against the crisis of 1690–1715; were these provinces still benefiting from the impetus of the very long period of recovery and reconstruction after the Thirty Years' War? Or did their peripheral position mean they escaped these typically French trends towards crisis? Or was there some other reason? It will be noticed that in Switzerland the curves of the tithe product or of cereal yields show hardly any sign of the 1690–1715 crisis.[16] Certainly Louis XIV was not king of Switzerland at the time! The Swiss cantons were lucky enough to avoid the bloody wars and high rates of taxation that France suffered during these decades. There were, of course, Swiss soldiers fighting in the French army at this period, but they were mercenaries.

Let us try to estimate the importance of the depression of 1690–1715. It was relatively slight in the countryside around Paris, where the sum derived from rents fell by only about 15%. But Paris had become rich, and its population had increased as a result of collecting taxes from all over France, the capital thus created around itself a privileged sector. Elsewhere, in the north and south of France the tithe and rents fell, in real terms, by between 25% and even 33%, depending on the region. This decline was not caused essentially by strikes: the period we are concerned with was in fact strongly Catholic (after the Revocation of the Edict of Nantes). The arguments – originally put forward by the Huguenots – which had been so powerful against the tithe in the sixteenth century had lost their force around 1700.

At this point I may be allowed to put forward an overall view. I have agreed with Bois and Neveux that cereal production in the sixteenth and seventeenth centuries never greatly exceeded a kind of ceiling which remained in place for several centuries. In *L'Histoire économique et sociale de la France*,[17] I put forward certain figures for this 'ceiling': 50 million quintals of grain in the area covered by

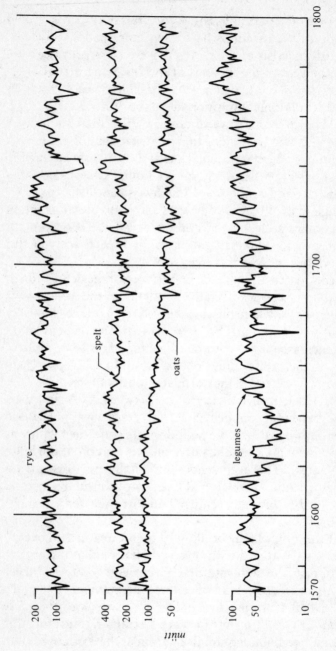

7. Grain tithes and yield ratios for the Zurich area, 1530–1800 (Head-Koenig)

present-day France at the beginning of the fourteenth century, and 60 million quintals during the long seventeenth century, starting from the ceiling of the decade 1550–60. There were, of course, significant fluctuations *below* this ceiling. At times both the population and cereal production were affected by some of these fluctuations which were long and far-reaching. This is to say no more than that the concept of 'fluctuation' is inseparable from that of 'equilibrium'. Chapters 5 and 6 dealt with a very long period of fluctuation which stretched from 1340 to 1550. The total population declined dramatically between 1340 and 1450; after this, between 1450 and 1550, it returned to approximately the levels of before the Black Death. In other words, the overall population of France (taking the area covered by contemporary France) went through a full circle: it plunged from about 17–19 million in 1330–40 to fewer than 10 million in 1450, then climbed again to 19 or even 20 million around 1550. This fluctuation could certainly be described as 'long'. The shattering of the equilibrium, then the return to stability took place over two centuries, from the 1340s to the 1550s. As we have seen, these phenomena also implied significant fluctuations in agricultural production, and especially in cereal production, which roughly kept pace with changes in the population. There was not always a very close parallel, however; in the long term, cereal production declined relatively more slowly than the population, around the middle of the fifteenth century.

I shall call this almost monstrous phenomenon a first-degree fluctuation. It was terribly dangerous and destructive. After 1550, and up until the present day, France was never again to suffer this type of fluctuation over two centuries. It is true that it is predicted by some people that the falling birth rate will bring a massive decline in the population at the end of the twenty-first century, but that, at least for the moment, is another story. As far as the period 1550–1720 is concerned, the overall population of France, especially in rural areas, remained static or even decreased by 10–20% during the worst periods, for example during the Wars of Religion or perhaps during the 1690s. It recovered later, and finally increased dynamically after 1720 so that the old ceiling – which for almost four centuries remained at the apparently insuperable level of 20 or 21 million – was exceeded. Between 1550 and 1800 it was impossible for the total 'French' population to decline by 50% or even more, as it had done in the period 1350–1450. If we are looking for real first-degree fluctuations in the 'modern' period we must look outside France, to Germany during the Thirty Years' War: during the years from 1630 to 1650 it is possible that the German population was reduced by 50%. It should be noted, too, that this disaster in Germany was spread over a shorter period than was the case in France during the Hundred Years' War. Moreover the very names 'Hundred Years' War' and 'Thirty Years' War' are enough to indicate the problem. We could say that the German disaster of the seventeenth century affected just *one* generation – extremely severely – rather than several.

Let us now consider, with respect to France, the difficult periods of the Wars of Religion, the 'Thirty Years' War–Fronde' period, and of the years 1690–1715: these wars had an effect on both the population and the cereal product, as well as on other variables. We could call them 'second-degree fluctuations'; they were significant, but less extensive and far-reaching than the first-degree fluctuations at the end of the Middle Ages.

Finally, after these first- and second-degree fluctuations come what I shall call 'third-degree fluctuations', which have been much studied by historians. These fluctuations involve sharp increases in mortality rates associated with epidemics and subsistence crises – which are of particular interest to the historian of agriculture. These crises were marked by a temporary shortage of grain; there would be a bad harvest (for example in 1709), which would be followed by a bread scarcity, itself brought about by high grain prices. Through poverty and epidemics, this grain shortage would help to provoke a high death rate for one or two years. On the whole, these third-degree fluctuations did not last long: they stretched over two or three years at the most. Their demographic impact was not enormous, even if their effects were cruel. Altogether, they killed at the most 'only' 10% or less of the population: this was perhaps the case in France in 1694.

The 'first-degree fluctuations' (the crises of the four-teenth and fifteenth centuries) have been studied from many angles. The third-degree fluctuations have also been the object of systematic research on the part of historians such as Meuvret, Goubert etc.[18] However, the second-degree, intermediate, fluctuations – those which lasted between one and four decades (like the Wars of Religion or the crisis at the end of Louis XIV's reign) and affected both the population and the agricultural economy – have not been studied as such, or at least not in a way which would combine the discovery of concrete facts with a general analysis of the phenomenon or the construction of an explanatory model. French society was affected by enor-mous second-degree fluctuations during the long seven-teenth century between 1550 and 1720. The first of these corresponds to the thirty-five years of the Wars of Religion, let us say from roughly 1560 to 1595; the second to the 'Thirty Years' War–Fronde' complex; and the third coin-cides with the last twenty-five years of Louis XIV's reign, 1690–1715.

During these three periods both the population and the agricultural product – especially cereals – suffered a decline, which could last for one decade, two or three decades or even longer. These negative phases were fol-lowed by periods of demographic and economic recovery – in the time of Henri IV and the young Louis XIII (1600–30); in the time of Colbert (1663–80); and in the time of Philippe d'Orleans and Cardinal Fleury (or after 1715 and during the 1720s and the 1730s). However, this last phase, the eighteenth century, was not just a period of recovery but of real growth: it took France 'through the looking glass' and created a different situation from that which had existed in the preceding three and a half centuries. Needless to say, the names of the ministers, kings and regents that I have listed here are purely symbolic; they are simply convenient labels for a period of recovery, or of relative prosperity. The internal social dynamic was, of course, a more important factor in these phases of agricultural or demographic recovery than the action of statesmen.

During the fifteen or sixteen decades which composed the 'long seventeenth century' (1560–1715) the positive and negative phases of the second-degree fluctuations were more or less evenly balanced: on the whole, this 'long seventeenth century' resulted in near stagnation. We cannot even totally dismiss the hypothesis that over this long period there was a slight increase in the population and in the cereal product. It is, however, true that developments in the urban sector could help to explain that increase, if it did occur.

This idea of progress in certain sectors leads us to some more general considerations. The seventeenth century was to some extent a period of economic semi-stagnation. But in France, even in agriculture, there were some signs of growth in certain isolated sectors. In the area around Toulouse, for example, the cultivation of maize, which had come from America via Spain, is mentioned for the first time in 1637. From 1653 onwards local production of maize was great enough to eradicate subsistence crises in this region; by 1675 maize already covered much the same area in the south-west of France as it did in 1900. It became a staple foodstuff for the peasants, a basis for making soup and other dishes. As a result, the peasants could sell their wheat to the neighbouring towns; and in the eighteenth century they exported it to the French Antilles. This meant that they came nearer to achieving a market economy. However, it is true that in France at this period maize was not yet as important as it was in Spain and Italy – it was a marginal and regional phenomenon. To illustrate this: in 1815 to 1840, according to the statistics, maize accounted for only 5% of all grain crops in France, while in the seventeenth century it was less than this. The same comments apply to silk, which during the seventeenth century became more important on both sides of the Rhône valley south of Lyons, but this localized expansion of silk production did not have a significant impact at the national level.

The vineyards in the south, however, underwent a real and significant growth in the seventeenth century. Vines replaced cereals, even on the fertile plains, and they covered 40% of the available valley land from 1627.[19] The expansion of wine production in Languedoc between 1600 and 1655 exceeded all previous ceilings; from the 1660s on, brandy was made in this region and exported, providing alternative outlets for the local vinegrowers who would otherwise have suffered from the decrease in prices. This was to become even more important when the Canal du Midi made it possible to import wheat from the Toulouse area into eastern Languedoc – from then on some wheat fields could be replaced with vines. Regional agriculture thus became more efficient by means of diversifying crops and by producing more valuable goods.

Here are a few figures relating to the Bordeaux wine industry:

Around 1300: 850,000 hectolitres of wine were exported.[20]

Around 1550: 212,000 hectolitres of wine were exported (during the Renaissance it was only in excessively good years that the old medieval ceiling of 850,000 hectolitres was attained).

In 1594–98: 255,000 hectolitres of wine were exported.

In 1637–40: 565,000 hectolitres of wine were exported, this being made up of 510,000 hectolitres of wine as such, and 55,000 hectolitres distilled into brandy.

Around 1700: 750,000 hectolitres of wine plus 168,000 hectolitres of brandy (distilled from 1,344,000 hectolitres of wine); or in other words, between two million and 2,100,000 hectolitres of wine, in various forms, were exported each year.

As far as the production and export of wine is concerned, the ceilings of the fourteenth century were at last exceeded around 1700; exports were then two and a half times greater than in 1300–10. The no-growth model which roughly applies to the population and to grains is thus far from being applicable to non-cereal products like wine. It is possible that situations similar to those which have been recorded at Bordeaux also occurred, though to a lesser extent, around towns like Nantes and La Rochelle. The figures we have for this region are less precise than for the Bordeaux area. We can in any case see the crucial importance of the Dutch practice of distilling wine to make spirits, which had spread to France in the sixteenth century, and in the seventeenth century it was a factor in the growth of the Atlantic provinces and their vineyards.

It is true that wine production did not increase everywhere in France in the seventeenth century: in the Angers area, there was simply a period of recovery between 1630 and 1640 which brought production back to the relatively high levels of before 1560.[21] After 1640 wine production in Anjou remained stable or even declined slightly for the rest of the long seventeenth century; the years 1690–1720 saw some severe crises (see Figure 8).

Further north and further east, however, the increase in population in Paris between 1660 and 1670–80 opened up the market: the capital accounted for 350,000 hectolitres of wine. This demand thus stimulated wine production which developed further south and as far as Beaujolais, thanks to the construction of canals which enabled wine to be transported to Paris from the new vineyards on the east of the Massif Central: *le Beaujolais nouveau est arrivé.*

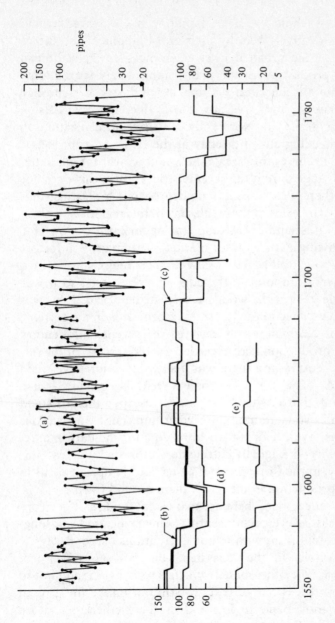

pipes

8. Wine production in Anjou, 1550–1790 (Garnier)

(a) = total wine production in pipes
(b) = weighted 10-year average (1640–9 = 100), for Pigeon, Terten-
tière, Fouassières, Pantière Léon, Fils de Prêtre, St Michel du
Terre

(c) = weighted 10-year average (1640–9 = 100), for Loisonnière, Piré,
Morin
(d) = 10-year average, area as (b)
(e) = 10-year average, area as (c)

On the whole, Paris, like London, slowly created around itself a relatively healthy division of labour.[22] The stimulation of the urban market encouraged specialization in cereal production in the plains immediately surrounding the capital; the rural sail-making industry was pushed further west, and especially into Maine. There was also a distinct trend in Normandy towards specialization in stockbreeding aimed directly at the Paris meat markets.[23] The tithe curves for cereals show a downward trend in the Pays d'Auge during the seventeenth century: this does not mean there was an economic depression! It was just that some of the fields of the fertile clay of this region were given over to grasslands, providing grazing for cattle destined for the growing Parisian meat market. Certain growth factors were more traditional. Many French regions were in a 'frontier' situation, on the edge of fine forests, so it was possible to clear the woods and create new fields. This was what happened in the Cotentin (a peninsula in the extreme west of Normandy): as early as the seventeenth century wheat production here exceeded the old records of the sixteenth century and there was a slow but impressive trend towards expansion. To some extent Normandy – like England, that greater Normandy – escaped the crisis and economic stagnation of the seventeenth century for various reasons: by developing stockbreeding for the Paris market in the Pays d'Auge; by cutting down forests for cereal production in the Cotentin; and by technical improvements in grain production in the fertile plain around Caen.

In France, then, there are two useful models of development in the seventeenth century. One is the model of long-term equilibrium with major fluctuations ('second-degree' fluctuations) in the ecosystem, but without much real increase. The other model, which is less obvious and not so widespread, is one of real growth, not unlike the growth which took place in England or the Netherlands. I am thinking of stockbreeding in Normandy and, in more Mediterranean style, of the expansion of wine-growing in

Bordeaux and of maize around Toulouse. There was also a third type of growth which was more traditional and seems almost medieval: this involved the clearing of the remaining forests in the Cotentin, and perhaps elsewhere – but this practice was not widespread.

The slight economic renaissance we have observed in France in the first half (or first third) of the seventeenth century had its counterparts in Belgium and Holland; but here the process was much more vigorous and innovative than in France.

In the Southern Netherlands (now Belgium) this revival was especially marked in Flanders, in the area around Brussels and in Brabant; it was, however, hindered by the wars which began in the Walloon areas in 1621. Very often, however, the high levels of the pre-war period were not equalled during the recovery in the 'Belgian' area. In Brabant, a decline of the towns weakened the market economy and discouraged the diversification of agriculture.[24] These negative influences remained, even though the total population increased to the point of stimulating traditional cereal production. The situation was much better in rural Flanders ('Belgian' Flanders today): there, specialization in the production of flax associated with the cottage spinning and weaving industries, reflects the permanent and very strong links between agriculture and the international market.[25] It was the only region in the Southern Netherlands 'which made progress during the first half of the seventeenth century, in terms of the productivity of the land': this increased productivity was a result of growth both in terms of value and of the amount produced.[26]

In the Northern Netherlands (the Netherlands as we know it), the Thirty Years' War did not have such a direct impact. The increase in revenue in real terms from 1580 to 1650–70 is therefore impressive. This was due, amongst other factors, to investment in various sectors: land reclamation, drainage, the construction of new buildings, the opening of canals and 'new techniques of intensive cultivation introduced into market gardening'. There was also, as Van der Wee points out, 'increased specialization', which stimulated productivity 'in terms of the amount and value of the products'. This specialization was made possible by importing grain from the Baltic countries which enabled the Dutch peasants to 'concentrate on dairy products, on horticulture and on crops required by industry', for example hops. These goods were aimed at the towns, where the population was increasing; the purchasing power of townspeople was often higher than that of the country folk. The diffusion of cottage industries in the countryside was another factor leading to higher rural incomes. This complex of factors has been described by the collective term 'Dutch husbandry'; it was to become popular in England after 1650, when it became mixed with native innovations. It is clear, then, that the records of the sixteenth century were decisively beaten in the Northern Netherlands in the seventeenth century 'in terms of increases in physical productivity and economic growth'.

Certain provinces in the Netherlands, however (for example Friesland, Groningen, Overijssel and Drenthe), were accustomed to selling cattle to the Germans. The crisis provoked in Germany by the Thirty Years' War led these Dutch provinces to switch over to dairy products.

In spite of this resounding success in the Netherlands in the first half of the seventeenth century, the second half was generally bad, or at least mediocre, not only in the Southern Netherlands but also in the Northern Netherlands. In the period 1650–1750 the Dutch – despite their previously brilliant agricultural performance – moved away from what was to become the English model, of a successful and expanding agriculture. Unfortunately for the Netherlands, they moved closer to the French model in the second half of the seventeenth century. We have already seen that in spite of certain fairly remarkable periods of recovery during Colbert's time, the rural economy in France was gravely affected by the severe crises of the mid and the very late seventeenth century; to such an extent that agricultural production in France was not really able to improve before 1715–20.

Belgium, like the north of France, had suffered badly as a result of the Thirty Years' War; its effects were felt in the 1620s and in the middle of the seventeenth century. The area also suffered from the various wars conducted by Louis XIV and his armies in the Netherlands: I am thinking, like Van der Wee, of the wars of 1667–8, 1672–8, 1688–97 and 1701–14, the last of which being the War of the Spanish Succession.[24] (See Figure 9.) The accompanying movement of population away from the towns and into the countryside (in spite of a certain increase in population here and there) had as a logical consequence the decline of the urban market. This meant that there could be no increase in the value of the goods produced; the marginal product of the farmers was close to zero, taking into account the fact that when there *was* a demographic expansion, this did not lead to an increase in the urban population.

The rural industries of Flanders were thus adversely affected by 'the collapse of colonial trade'. In the Northern Netherlands, according to Van der Wee, rents, which had risen before 1650 tended to level out after this date, and even to fall after 1670. One factor in this depression was the decline in urban demand for expensive foodstuffs like 'crops for processing, horticultural produce and dairy produce'. This decline in urban demand was itself provoked or aggravated by several political and other factors, such as:

(a) the end of colonial and commercial expansion in the Netherlands,

(b) the high tariffs imposed by other countries, which limited Dutch exports,

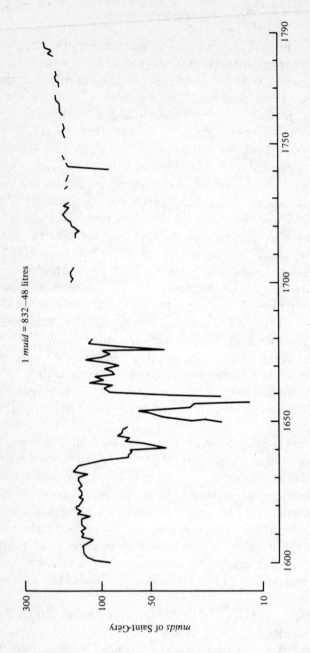

1 *muid* = 832—48 litres

9. Income from eight wheat tithes paid to the church of Saint-Géry in Cambrai, 1600—1790 (Neveux, *Les grains du Cambrésis*, Paris, 1980, p.63)

(c) the high price of labour in Dutch towns. This was itself the result of, amongst other factors, the strength of the guilds.

In the Northern Netherlands, as in France, high taxation in the countryside was also a factor in the difficulties facing the peasant economy in the second half of the seventeenth century. In spite of some progress in rural industries in certain regions of the Netherlands, the second half of the seventeenth century and the beginning of the eighteenth century were not, on the whole, a prosperous period in most of these regions, just as they had not been in France (with the exception in this case of the Colbert years, which were, as we have seen, reasonably prosperous).

Let us now look at Italy: according to Aymard, in Sicily, and perhaps more generally in southern Italy, the crisis at the end of the sixteenth century was more or less over by 1610. However, the recovery started from fairly low levels and lacked dynamism. It was to continue in a relatively lethargic way until the middle of the seventeenth century. 'It was linked to an attempt to restructure the organization of production, which became more oppressive.' The wealthier farmers (the equivalent of the French *laboureurs* or the English yeomen) known locally as *massari* or *borgesi*, lost their security of tenure. The great landowners and their managers practised usury at the expense of the peasants. Rents and taxes were increased. The peasants were weakened by this intense exploitation and the period of recovery thus came to an end, finished off by the bad harvests of 1646 and the dreadful plague of 1656.[27]

In Sicily it is true that the highest demographic peak came around 1680–90, but the population was largely rural; we find once again certain phenomena which were noted in a different context by Van der Wee when he was discussing Belgian Brabant in the same period. The lack of agricultural diversification meant that the goods produced did not increase in value. Restrained by the new trends of the seventeenth century, urbanization in Sicily, as in the Belgian province, ceased to have a beneficial influence on agriculture. The market economy was weakened: sugar exports reached a ceiling in 1670–80 and then ceased (was this already the result of competition from the European colonies in America?). Silk exports from Sicily reached a ceiling in 1670–80.[28] Cereal exports were 10 to 20% lower than they had been in the sixteenth century. It should be remembered that during the second half or the last third of the seventeenth century a certain number of countries which had been accustomed to exporting grain experienced difficulties and cereal exports were reduced. England, however, escaped this crisis – her wheat exports to foreign countries increased.

The situation around 1680, then, was rather bad. However, a new period of recovery became evident from 1680–90. Like the one which had preceded it from 1610 on, this revival involved a restructuring of the economy. But this time the process was different and took place on two different levels: the economic revival in Sicily and southern Italy which began around 1690, at a time when France was facing a serious crisis, above all affected small family subsistence farms. These farmers benefited from the low rents that the crisis forced the landlords to accept, forcing them to become less greedy than in the past. In certain cases, new family subsistence farms, with almost complete ownership leases, were created by the *seigneurs*; these grants are typical of periods of repopulation in the Middle Ages as well as the modern period, in France as well as in Italy.[29] The rise of small, almost independent farms 'stimulated an increase in the gross product by developing a subsistence–oriented polyculture, which also produced a surplus for the market'. Thus, according to Aymard,[30] the period 1690–1710, which was so harsh in France, was also relatively difficult in Italy: but the agricultural structures based on the family smallholding survived this bad period with the minimum of damage. From 1710 onwards the great estates began to expand – they developed a more enlightened management and were increasingly oriented towards the market. From then on Italy adjusts more or less to the model of European agricultural growth in the eighteenth century (see the next chapter).

This applies to southern Italy, but what was the position with regard to the rest of the country? According to Aymard and Basini, after the period of stabilization or even economic crisis in the seventeenth century there was a new period of expansion, or at least of recovery, which began around 1690; this was to continue throughout the eighteenth century, despite various setbacks and differences in timing between the two sectors – the family farm and the great estates.[31]

As far as Spain is concerned, Gonzalo Anes Alvarez does not believe in the 'general crisis of the seventeenth century': he sees this period as one of stabilization and not one in which there was an overall demographic decline throughout Spain. It was also a period of readjustment. Certain towns like Madrid, Cadiz and the cities of Andalusia were developing, and this led to a more rational distribution of population, as a result of a 'rural exodus' (see the similar phenomena in the Paris region which have been studied by Jean Jacquart).[32] Grain yields were increased by concentrating production on the least marginal lands. Maize production was expanding. The abandoning of cereal production on marginal lands encouraged a certain increase in stockbreeding: these arable lands were converted into pastures. The additional cattle consumed more secondary cereals, such as barley and oats, so that the proportion of these cereals in the overall grain production increased at the expense of wheat. The seventeenth century was thus not a period of severe economic crisis in Spain, though there were difficult times in certain crucial decades, especially during the first half or the first two thirds of the century; it was rather a period of stabilization, normalization and reorganization.

To define more precisely the trends of the seventeenth century in Spain I shall now take a few regional examples. In Valencia there was a distinct decline in cereal production after 1600–10; the expulsion of the Moors was only one of several causes. The lowest point of this crisis in Valencia was reached around 1647–9, at the time of a serious outbreak of plague. If one gives the year 1610 an index of 100, the grain tithe fell to 53 in 1640–50. From 1680 on there were already signs of a recovery, which can be compared with that taking place in Catalonia, also during the 1680s – even though here the wars at the end of Louis XIV's reign were to have a temporarily disastrous effect.[33] In Murcia in the south-east of Spain there was a decline in cereal production between 1604 and 1669; there was then a rather exceptional period of recovery, followed by a period of expansion between 1670 and 1730, 'a fine start to the eighteenth century', as Guy Lemeunier remarks. In Lower Andalusia, cereal yields were low between 1600 and 1670, but rose distinctly from 1670 to about 1700, after which these increases were consolidated.[34]

In Galicia, the economic crisis occurred exactly between 1615 and 1645.[35] A recovery took place from 1645 to 1675 (a period when the cereal tithe increased by 8%), and it became stronger between 1672 and 1730 (an increase of 19%). After 1670 maize played an important part in this recovery which resulted in a period of positive growth.

In the Basque country, the economic crisis occurred in the first half of the seventeenth century, between 1610 and 1640, during which period the overall volume of the grain tithe declined by 19%.[36] The subsequent period of recovery/growth was particularly dynamic since it was an area stimulated by the international sea trade: between 1650 and 1720 cereal production possibly increased three fold (see Figure 5). One would think this was England … Maize (which was of no importance in England!) was an extremely important factor in this expansion in the Basque economy. Wine-growing was also important; Basque wine production was multiplied by 2.8 between 1615 and 1715 (see similar phenomena further north in Languedoc and especially in the Bordeaux area). Agriculture in the Basque country was thus efficiently restructured: the exploitation of marginal lands on the hillsides was more or less abandoned, the victim of a 'classic' long seventeenth-century economic crisis, from 1615 to 1715. But the particular difficulties of this area – in the hillsides and marginal lands – should not prevent us from recognizing the overall vigorous expansion which took place. We should not fail to see the wood for the trees.

These Spanish trends cannot be separated from the parallel and contemporary trends in Latin America. In Mexico the tithe product went through a period of crisis around 1650 but it began to recover very rapidly from 1670 as a result of wasteland clearance or the taking of other new land into cultivation. The fundamental explanation for these trends was a demographic one. The Mexican population reached its lowest point in the middle of the seventeenth century; then, after 130 disastrous years, it finally began to recover.

I do not have much data for Germany. The Thirty Years' War was, of course, a major catastrophe; it reduced cereal production by at least 50%. We can imagine its effects by looking at the curves for Alsace, which was also devastated by war. When the war was over, there was a distinct recovery in the last forty years of the seventeenth century.

In England the period 1650–1720 was marked by five trends: (a) advances in agricultural technology, (b) a population increase which was neither excessive nor dangerous, (c) a steadily increasing demand for a variety of foodstuffs, (d) increased grain exports, (e) an increasing domestic and total supply of foodstuffs, even when calculated on a per capita basis.[37]

These comparisons put the economic growth of England between 1650 and the eighteenth century in a different light: the British immunity to the so-called 'general crisis of the seventeenth century' no longer appears as a miraculous island in a sea of European stagnation and depression, but rather as a particularly privileged instance of expansion within the framework of the general stabilization of the seventeenth century. Other examples of expansion or recovery emerged on the Continent at the same time, though these, it is true, turned out to be less important. The period of expansion in England after 1650 was paralleled (and supported) on the other side of the Channel (and on the other side of the Atlantic). There were certain simultaneous positive trends, for example in Germany after 1660; in Spain and Latin America (not to mention North America) after 1670; and in Italy after 1690. It remains to be seen whether these positive trends reacted on one another; the possibility of a profitable interaction between the different instances of expansion seems a reasonable hypothesis, at least as far as the Atlantic countries are concerned. I am thinking of North and South America; and of the existence of centres of growth like Bordeaux and Saint-Malo on the western coast of France, both of which may have owed something to the English expansion. As for Spain itself, the economic growth which she achieved, especially after 1670, was not totally independent from the growth which was to take place in Italy after 1690.

France, too, enjoyed some relatively prosperous periods after 1650, essentially from 1662 to the 1680s. However, Holland – and to a much more tragic extent, Poland and Hungary – suffered a bad period in the second half of the seventeenth century; in central Europe it reached disaster levels. In the Netherlands, though, there had been plenty of time in the first half of the seventeenth century to develop the techniques of 'Dutch husbandry'. After 1650 this model was to be transmitted to England, where it was combined with local innovations. Dutch husbandry had taken root in the sector of small, family farms in Holland; it was later to work wonders at the level of the huge British estates, where they knew how to combine the advantages of large-scale farming with the sophisticated mini-technology from the Netherlands. In Poland, the decline in grain exports from the Baltic to the Netherlands was partly the result of war damage. This decline created a vacuum which absorbed the expanding exports of grain from England after 1660. This was one of the factors which contributed to the rise of the agricultural product in England in the second half of the seventeenth century. Poland's misfortune was England's luck.

It can be seen from this analysis that the idea of a general crisis of the seventeenth century cannot be accepted as such, and that it would be better described as a period of stabilization. Let us leave agricultural problems for a moment, and look, with Morineau, at the trade across the Atlantic between Spain and her colonies in the seventeenth century.[38] The increase in the value of the goods transported by sea from Spain to the New World compensates for the decrease in the quantity transported. Cargoes of precious metals from the silver mines of the New World also went through 'a marked decline around 1640 and especially around 1650 ... owing to the wars which hindered the Atlantic sea trade'. However, apart from this bad period, the cargoes of bullion were still at quite a high level between 1630 and 1640, and again after 1660 until 1700 and beyond. The levels were comparable to those of the sixteenth century. It seems, then, that the 'crisis' of the seventeenth century – if there was such a crisis – was not the result of a lack of metal for the production of coins. There were, of course, periods of economic and demographic decline in various European countries. As far as the Continent is concerned, this long seventeenth century appears rather to have been marked by a series of conscious or unconscious processes tending towards the adjustment, stabilization and normalization of the economy; it was not without periods of expansion in certain regions or certain sectors.

8

The eighteenth century:
economic take-off?

After 1670 in Spain and after 1715 in France there was very distinct increase in the agricultural product. This rise was paralleled by a certain increase in population. In France, and perhaps in other Western European countries as well, this economic revival was particularly significant. From the 1320s to the end of the seventeenth century it seems that the population of France scarcely exceeded a maximum of 20 or 21 million inhabitants. In the eighteenth century, for the first time, this figure was to be substantially surpassed: around 1788–9 the population of France reached 27 million. This demographic development clearly provided a very positive stimulus to agricultural production. However, if one looks at agricultural growth in the eighteenth century over the whole of Central and Western Europe, then the factors responsible for this growth seem less obvious and more divergent than they had been between 1450 and 1560. One of the indications is that the demographic trends underlying the agricultural expansion were not the same. In the eighteenth century the population rose less dramatically, in percentage terms, than it had done during the period from 1450 to 1550. In France in this earlier period the population had increased by 100% or possibly more, whereas it rose by only 29% between 1700 and 1789. Generally speaking, agriculture did not expand in a uniform manner during the eighteenth century. There are countries such as Hungary where there does not appear to have been any growth; regions, like Brittany, where agriculture remained stagnant; and countries where growth slowed down or even stopped in certain provinces from 1750 to 1760 (this was often the case in Spain, Portugal and to some extent Italy). Finally, there were regions where expansion was maintained at an impressive level from the beginning of the century to the end: this was true for England if not always for France.

It may be interesting to start with Hungary, which did not follow the common growth pattern of the eighteenth century.[1] There was in fact no increase in cereal production in Hungary in the eighteenth century – there was merely a period of recovery or stagnation, followed by a further severe decline at the end of the eighteenth century. Hungarian historians, such as László Makkai and Istvan Kiss, do not always agree about the causes of this trend. They seem to think that the eighteenth century was not in fact a crisis period for the Hungarian economy, but rather a time when there was a certain degree of expansion compared with the stagnation or even decline of the seventeenth century. It must be admitted that the Hungarian grain tithes do not always reflect the overall economic situation with regard to agriculture. One way or another many peasants managed to avoid paying these tithes and to get themselves exempted, for example by cultivating land not liable to tithes. The production of goods which were exempt (such as maize, potatoes, wine and cattle) shows a distinct increase during the eighteenth century. At this period, then, rather than undergoing a crisis (which was hardly typical of the eighteenth century), Hungarian agriculture diversified, and so did consumption – there was an increase in meat consumption in particular. Rather like France during the prosperous 1460s, Hungary was not yet really suffering from the problems of overpopulation: in the eighteenth century it was relatively underpopulated. Meat consumption was all the more important because the land which had not grown cereals since the seventeenth century could easily be used as pasture for sheep and cattle.

Hungary, unlike other European countries which underwent a dramatic expansion throughout their agricultural sectors, including cereal production, offers us the model of a diversification of production without any noticeable increase in the amount of grain produced.

In Poland there was a distinct period of recovery which began around 1720 and continued until the 1790s at least. The trends in Polish agriculture were thus rather like those present in countries further to the west, like France and Germany. In this respect, Poland was quite unlike Hungary. It was, if I may say so, less 'eastern'. However, the increase in grain production in Poland in the eighteenth century did not amount to a real breakthrough, as in England and probably France: it was more a question of recovering the high levels of production which had already been reached around the 1570s. Moreover this recovery was not complete; it only reached 90% of the levels of the 1570s. As a result the per capita grain ration which was in theory available for each inhabitant of Poland remained lower, in 1790, than it had been during the prosperous 1560s and 1570s. By ignoring the figures for oats and calculating this ration in wheat, barley and rye, the following results are obtained: in 1789 the theoretical cereal ration per head was 261 kg, whereas in 1570 it had been 382 kg.[2] These figures are, of course, purely theoretical: in fact, part of this grain was exported and part was used as animal feed. They still give some idea of the limits to agricultural expansion in Poland during the eighteenth century.

Let us now look at the part of Europe which followed a more classic pattern of development. The eighteenth-century English expansion has been carefully studied by English historians.[3] It was partly the result of technical improvements: the English adopted new plants or at least cultivated more widely those that were already known, such as turnips and various types of crops for fodder and for industrial use; they also irrigated the meadows. Cereal production itself rose for various reasons, in response to the increased demand from the home market, and as a result of grain exports which became very important from the 1660s on. The movement towards enclosure, which led to increased agricultural production, accelerated after 1750. In spite of this remarkable progress, the increase in population, which was particularly pronounced after 1750, did for a while lend a certain reality to the pessimistic theories of Malthus, which were undoubtedly relevant for Great Britain, at least until the beginning of the nineteenth century.[4] According to Deane and Cole, wheat production in England increased by 34.5% between 1700 and 1790, and most of this took place after 1740; the rise in population over this period was a little higher, 41.5%.[5] This gap between the increase in cereal production and the increase in population is described by the famous Malthusian scissors: they open when the population increases at a greater rate than the means of subsistence. This was one of the causes of the rise in grain prices in Great Britain after 1740 – a rise which was paralleled elsewhere in Western Europe, especially in France.

Was the trend very different in Ireland? Thanks to Dickson, the rise in rents in Ireland between 1700–20 and 1770–90 is well documented.[6] He has made use of the figures for the price of butter to express the increase in real terms – since stockbreeding was particularly important in Ireland, butter prices are probably more suitable than grain prices for this statistical operation. In 70 years rents in Ireland rose by 82% in real terms. This increase cannot be separated from an increase in agricultural production, which owes a great deal to the ease with which new land could be brought into cultivation: in Ireland much of the cultivated land bordered fallow or marshes. In addition to this rise in the volume of the agricultural product, other factors stimulated the economy and thus contributed to this increase in rents: these included the introduction of potato farming and the rising population. The increase in rents led to the division of holdings, and even of great estates. The landowners took advantage of the situation to 'turn the screw' on their tenants by forcing them to pay higher rents.

Let us now look at the Netherlands, starting with the area covered by present-day Belgium. According to Van der Wee, the new period of Austrian domination coincided there with 'a sharp upturn in agriculture and a remarkable expansion which, so far as production and the productivity of the land was concerned, was sometimes just a matter of recovering previous levels'. This increase followed the difficult age of Louis XIV; it began at various dates in different regions, but all around 1750. The end of the War of the Austrian Succession around the middle of the eighteenth century marked the beginning of a particularly rapid period of expansion for Belgian agriculture, which began with a period of recovery, and went on to real growth. At this point, Van der Wee is confronted by the theories of Morineau, Vandenbroecke and Verderpijpen, as well as the ideas of Neveux, who sees the problem from a slightly different angle. According to Vandenbroecke and Verderpijpen, 'if one takes the grain yields as an index, one should be careful not to overestimate the extent of the revival in agricultural production in Belgium in the eighteenth century; in fact it was merely a matter of restoring the maximum levels which had already been reached in the thirteenth and fourteenth centuries'.[7] To be more precise, the thesis of Vandenbroecke and Verderpijpen can be summarized in the following three propositions:

(a) in the prosperous regions, for example around Brussels, the high yields of 19 to 20 hectolitres to the hectare which were achieved around 1800 had already been reached during the fourteenth and fifteenth centuries.

(b) In less well-cultivated areas, however (for example le Métier de Furnes), the wheat yields only reached 10 to 11 hectolitres per hectare in the first half of the seventeenth century. Around 1800 higher yields (20 to 21 hectolitres to the hectare) were at last achieved in this region. The same applies to the area around Bruges, though over a longer period: from 1400 to 1800. It appears, then, that the real agricultural revolution in Belgium consisted in the following: regional differences disappeared; and cereal yields in most regions reached the record levels previously achieved only in the most dynamic areas.

(c) The increase in population in Belgium in the eighteenth century made it necessary to turn to other sources of food. In fact, as a result of the limitations already mentioned, cereal production in general (and wheat production in particular) could not keep pace, and substitutes such as potatoes had to be found.

Let us now try to strike a balance. It is possible that, as Neveux suggests, the production of grain by traditional methods managed by the end of the eighteenth century to recover the levels that had already been achieved at the beginning of the fourteenth century, before the Black Death. But we should not be too pessimistic; the Belgians, fortunately for them, had other resources during the eighteenth century: the introduction of potato farming on a very large scale in the eighteenth century was the most significant innovation, and it soon increased agricultural productivity in terms of calorific value, and even in terms of monetary value. Since supply and demand both increased, dairy farming and horticulture also became important at this period. Wealth in general increased as a result of the expansion of the textile industry based on linen, cotton and hemp production. Cottage industries also expanded, as well as the coalmining and the metal industries. This took place in Wallonia, of course, but also – apart from heavy industry – in Brabant, in Flanders and around Antwerp. The new proletariat, or semi-proletariat, created by this development of industry and traditional crafts did not make a fortune; but, together with their employers, large and small, they fostered an increased demand for agricultural products. This resulted in an increase in the production of fodder crops, clover and beet in those regions. The Polder regions, on the other hand, retained a more traditional pattern of agricultural production.

Let us now look at the area known today as the Netherlands, where the pattern of its development was the reverse of that of the South. At first, during an initial 'golden age' (during the first half of the seventeenth century), the Northern Netherlands were prosperous and the South was in a more difficult position.[8] In the eighteenth century the opposite was true; the North now trailed behind England and Belgium as far as agricultural progress was concerned. Belgium, as we have just seen, achieved fairly good results; her agricultural performance was stimulated as a side effect of a new type of industrial growth, based on coal etc. The very different situation in the North can be seen from the graph for agricultural income and rents (expressed in terms of quantities of cheese) in the Northern Netherlands for the whole of the eighteenth century.[9] These graphs do not even reach the peaks of the 1650s. The Northern Netherlands were no longer able to achieve significant agricultural progress, after their extraordinary 'leap forward' during the first half of the seventeenth century. Although the introduction of the potato increased productivity during the eighteenth century, the new, real agricultural revolution had to wait for the introduction of new scientific methods (such as chemical fertilizers and machinery), which were not really to appear till the nineteenth century. Belgium, on the other hand, having been slower to develop in the seventeenth century, retained certain reserves of productivity, within the framework of the old-style technology, on which it was possible to draw in the eighteenth century.

So far as Italy is concerned, we have already seen that the crisis, or at least the difficult period of the seventeenth century, made way for recovery or even growth from the 1690s on. However, the increase in production in Italy could not be compared with what was achieved in England and also, to a lesser extent, in France. In Italy, growth was not sustained throughout the eighteenth century: around

1750–60, as in many parts of Spain, the relatively modest growth of the eighteenth century slowed down or even stopped altogether. Thus a cycle of expansion, which had not in any case been very pronounced, came to an end, at least temporarily. In northern Italy the exceptional areas in which agriculture was still expanding after 1750–60 were nearly always the areas involved to some extent in drainage or irrigation schemes. It was possible to increase the acreage available for grain and thus increase production – by constructing a canal system to irrigate the land where water was short, or to drain it where water was excessive. As for the more general obstacles to the growth of cereal production, they were bypassed by the introduction of new crops such as rice and maize.[10] These two crops did indeed become very important in northern Italy in the eighteenth century. In a region like Piedmont, where agriculture was relatively well developed, there was an impressive increase in the production of rice, maize and wheat between 1745 and 1780.[11] Agriculture was also diversified by the development of vines and olives. Similarly, the coastal area of Apulia was transformed by the planting of extensive olive groves; and some plains were irrigated and planted with orange trees. Basically, these developments in Italy were not unlike the diversification and intensification of agriculture by means of irrigation which Pierre Vilar has described for Catalonia at the same period.[12]

Italy's agricultural production was also diversified by the development of profitable crops, such as saffron and especially silk, for use in industry. According to Carlo Poni, in certain areas of north and central Italy silk production increased four fold between the sixteenth and the eighteenth centuries.[13] In 1781 more silk was being spun in Italy than cotton in England! This expansion in silk production was particularly important in northern Italy in the eighteenth century, but not in the south: there silk production had reached its ceiling in the middle of the seventeenth century.

However, the process of de-industrialization which was taking place in Italy meant that the silk was exported in the form of thread. The situation was thus not the same as during the great boom in Italian silk in the seventeenth century, when the product was exported at a much later stage of processing, in other words as woven material or finished articles. In Italy in the eighteenth century, then, the expansion in *agriculture* was unfortunately matched by a decline in *industry*. One of the secrets of British predominance at this period was precisely the fact that in Great Britain agriculture and industry managed to develop at the same time.

The modest improvements in agricultural performance that were achieved in Italy in the eighteenth century were based on a Latin, Mediterranean type of agriculture dating back to ancient Rome and to classical agronomists such as Columella, Cato and a few others; silk farming, however, was introduced only in the Middle Ages. This type of agriculture, classical and medieval in origin, was capable of spasmodic phases of expansion during periods of population growth along the northern coasts of the Mediterranean. It was well established and efficient, concentrating largely on vines and olives. It may be compared with the type of agriculture to be found in the Netherlands, North and South. This type was developed much later, between the fifteenth and the seventeenth centuries, and it proved to be even more efficient than the Latin model and more capable, in the distant future, of improvement by scientific methods.

Let us now look at the various regions of Italy, starting from the south and moving north. In the south the process of diversification that I have mentioned met certain obstacles. The very large estates or *latifundia* concentrated exclusively on grain production; they therefore suffered from periodic slumps which slowed down or halted the expansion of cereal production. In some cases, however, diversification was possible within this framework, provided that it

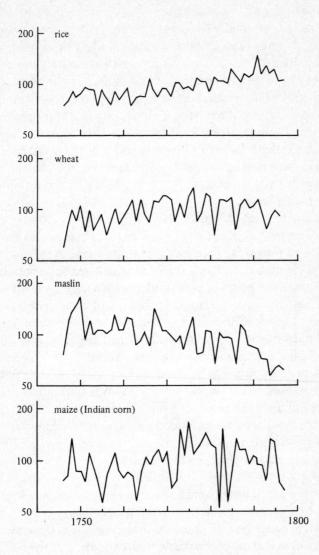

10. Agricultural production in Italian Piedmont, 1746–97 (Davico)

was eroded: the *latifundia* were in fact partly dismembered or divided into smallholdings farmed for subsistence by means of emphyteosis contracts (very long-term or hereditary leases granted to a peasant family in return for low rents). In these cases, the new smallholders (leaseholders) could diversify by extending the cultivation of vines and olives etc. In the last chapter we saw that from the 1690s on there had been certain signs of recovery in the agriculture of southern Italy, a recovery which took place at the level of the small family farm. Such farms had benefited from the economic depression in Europe in so far as the great estates which exported grain had suffered from the decline in demand: this, paradoxically, gave the small family holdings their chance.

According to Maurice Aymard, however, the great southern estates, or *latifundia*, reasserted themselves from 1700–10 onwards. This was particularly true in the case of the great estates of the Jesuits for which we have detailed accounts: the good fathers tended to manage their affairs well and to make precise calculations of their profits and losses. They tried to achieve a better balance between input and output. To do this they developed the vineyards, the olive plantations etc., as well as raising cattle. Cereals, however, continued to be the most important product from their estates. 'They marketed their goods with great care; consequently the income from the farm, or simply the profit from the business tended to leave rents behind, in the case of both the small, family subsistence farms and the great estates like those of the Jesuits.'[14]

After 1750–60, however, this new type of expansion or recovery based on income and profit came to an end. A new phase of economic stability or even depression appears to have been reached. In southern Italy there was once again an economic crisis comparable to the situation at the end of the sixteenth century or the middle of the seventeenth century. The economic problems in southern Italy in the second half of the eighteenth century are paralleled by the sharp decline in cereal yields in 1762–79 on the great estates of the Roman Campagna.[15]

According to our sources, the causes of this halt to growth was as follows:

(1) The increase in population which took place in the towns and in the country in the first half of the eighteenth century tended to 'exert pressure which increased both rents and the taxes levied by the State and the town authorities on the rural population'.[16] We do not need to stress this point. It is well known that an increase in population does indeed tend to produce an increase in the rents paid by the peasants, because of the increased competition for leases on any particular estate. This explains, for example, the crisis in cereal production in Apulia around 1770. The rise in population in general, and in the urban population in particular, resulted in increased demand. This caused grain prices to rise too quickly; the small peasants, who were not self-sufficient, were thus in a difficult situation: they had trouble making ends meet and buying the grain essential for their own, and their family's, survival.

(2) Aymard thinks that another factor was the exhaustion of the land, especially of the marginal lands which were cultivated too intensely; the drastic reduction in the periods when the land was allowed to lie fallow could result in a series of poor harvests.

(3) The small, family subsistence farms had been subdivided to a dangerous level, so that they were no longer viable. Once again, this was a classic Malthusian situation (see previous chapters).

What is more, the great landowners showed signs of regression towards an archaic form of agriculture. They tended to abandon the most enlightened forms of management, which had been practised during the good years 1710–50, since these methods appeared to be less and less profitable, despite their striking modernity. The new climate of depression and pessimism which spread during the second half of the eighteenth century was not conducive to methods like these. The great landowners and their agents often reverted to straightforward exploitation of the peasants by means of usury, high rents and sometimes even by increasing certain seigneurial dues such as *terrages* or *champarts*. It is the classic solution – to turn the screw. Sometimes these great landowners moved over from cereal production to stockraising, which seemed more profitable in the particular conditions of the period. These changes also helped to flatten the curves for grain production, or even to depress them.

North of Rome, however, the system of sharecropping or *mezzadria*, which was later to be considered archaic, showed considerable flexibility in the eighteenth century and made possible the diversification of agriculture. The produce of 'diversified' agriculture – wine, silk, hemp and linen – was particularly important to the sharecropper. The towns had a significant influence here – though sometimes underdeveloped, they were an important feature of Italian economic development. Sharecropping, especially in central Italy, forged a link between the leading citizens of Bologna (say), or Padua, who were also landowners, and the peasants, who were lessees or sharecroppers.

Further north, in the valley of the Po, the eighteenth century looks very modern. The estates were relatively large and were managed in an up-to-date way. 'Urban capital meant that it was possible to introduce irrigation and drainage schemes, to produce fodder crops, and to develop stockbreeding to provide both meat and dairy produce for the market.'[17] The Veneto was another area which developed the raising of dairy cattle in the eighteenth century. More generally, Maurice Aymard has tried to establish the relative proportion of grain in the overall agricultural product in the various regions of Italy: this amounts to 80–90% in the south; but perhaps only 45% in the north. The periodic recessions in cereal production, especially after 1750–60, posed more of a threat in the south than in the north.

The eighteenth century

The decisive factor in many regions of Italy was still the slowing down or interruption of growth after 1750–60. Did the fact that the peasants were in debt contribute to this situation in the area around Ravenna? Around the middle of the century this indebtedness became more and more severe, especially amongst the sharecroppers; it could have been one of the factors which put an end to the period of expansion.[18]

It will be noticed that historians of Italy, whichever side of the Alps they come from, stress the importance of the fact that the peasants were overwhelmed by a system of exploitation which increased in cycles. This, amongst other things, would explain their incapacity to sustain growth above a certain level and over a certain period (both limited). In spite of significant developments in some regions, especially in the north, Italy after 1750 was 'closer to a model of recession than to a model of take-off and sustained growth'. According to Aymard, Italy was 'on the conceptual periphery of the take-off model', a model which is relevant further north, in France and especially in England. France was half way between an agrarian capitalism based on expansion (fully exemplified by Great Britain) and an agrarian capitalism based on 'simple survival and reproduction', typical of the Mediterranean countries. This second 'ideal type' was to be found particularly in the south of Italy: the essential task of such a 'mode of production' was to supply the urban markets – in other words, to feed the cities. It did make a profit, but still did not achieve sustained growth. The great estates of southern Italy were, par excellence, the prototypes of this second brand of capitalism, distinctly more traditional than the first.[19]

In Spain, as in France and England, the essential feature of the eighteenth century was the increase in population. Over the whole century the population of Spain probably increased by between 40 and 45% – a rate similar to that in England and higher than in France. 'This demographic expansion was greater on the coasts than in the interior of the peninsula.'[20] The population increase meant that new land was brought, or brought back, into cultivation 'because of the increase in the active rural population'. Here and there productivity increased in certain sectors, thanks to the introduction of turnips and especially maize. In Valencia and Lerida new lands were irrigated. However, the main increase in the agricultural product and in the area brought back into cultivation was achieved on the marginal lands which were often some distance from the centres of production. The fact that these new fields were far away and not very fertile led to a decline in productivity, both in relation to the land and to the individual farmer. At the same time, because the lands were marginal and because of the increase in population and hence in demand, the price of staple foods was increasing, as in France and in England. The grazing lands available for the plough teams were reduced as new land was taken over for cereals. The peasants then came to use more and more mules in the plough teams, but the problem was that these animals consumed secondary cereals which were more expensive to produce than grass. In the end, on the poor lands the use of hundreds and hundreds of mules meant that production costs tended to exceed the market price of the grain. This limiting factor was one of the problems which put an end to the 'great cycle of agrarian expansion' in the second half of the eighteenth century.[21] When trying to explain why this long period of expansion came to an end, Aymard particularly stresses the exploitation of the peasant in Italy, whereas for Spain Anes concentrates on the fact that it was not physically possible to take much new land into cultivation. These interpretations may not be mutually exclusive.

Since for Spain we do not have any studies comparable to those of Morineau, we can assert with some confidence, along with Anes, that there was a distinct increase in cereal production in Spain during the eighteenth century, even if this increase did not keep pace with the increase in population. In most cases the ceilings for cereal production which were reached between 1730 and 1780 were higher than those which had been reached in the seventeenth century.

The most remarkable fact is that the 'eighteenth-century' expansion began rather early in Spain, around 1670. In many cases it also fizzled out rather early, around 1730–60. The peak, which was followed by a decline, was reached around 1730 in Murcia, and around 1760 in Galicia. However, in the most favourably situated areas, notably along the coasts, the expansion continued until about 1790, as it did in Catalonia and around Granada.

In the Basque country there was a vigorous expansion in the coastal regions, and this often lasted until around 1770. Production was very much higher than it had been in the seventeenth century, and this was true for vines as well as for grain and maize; wine consumption almost entirely replaced that of traditional Basque cider, previously produced from local apples.

In Galicia Eiras Roel has noted a long phase of expansion over a century or rather more – from 1645 to 1760. For cereals, the eighteenth-century ceilings were 47% higher than those of the seventeenth century. The increase is particularly marked in the humid coastal areas where maize and cattle raising were particularly important; at this period each family farm had on average three oxen. In the last third of the eighteenth century there was a period of depression, or at least of stabilization.

Around Segovia or Old Castille the eighteenth-century expansion largely took the form of the production of secondary cereals for animal fodder; the local towns were too impoverished to stimulate the cultivation of wheat.

In the province of Murcia the great period of growth in cereal production – wheat, then barley – was between 1670 and 1730. In the second half of the eighteenth century there were already signs of a depression.

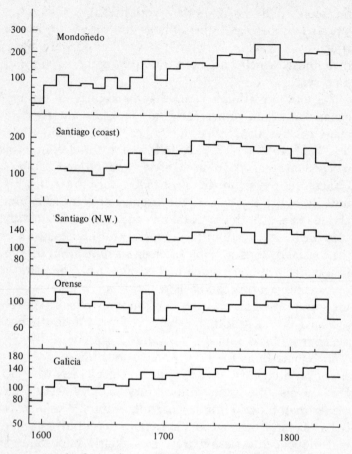

11. Grain tithes in Galicia, 1600–1837 (Eiras Roel)

Around Malaga the peak came about 1750. After this there was a decline: the more dynamic coastal zones continued to expand till about 1775; the interior regions stopped around 1730.

Ponsot has carried out some remarkable research for western Andalusia.[22] To quote Anes Alvarez once more: 'In this region, if we are to trust the evidence of the tithes, the production of wheat increased vigorously from about 1712–15 ... This expansion seemed to stop at the end of the eighteenth century but appearances were deceptive –

the pause was due more to a diversification of production than to a real crisis. In fact the numbers of cattle in the mountains increased, and so did vine production in the lowlands.'[23] Grain yields, however, declined after 1740 until 1780, after which they rose again until 1800.

In the kingdom of Valencia the increase in production and in rents lasted until around 1770, and seems to have been especially pronounced during the 1760s. In Catalonia, Pierre Vilar has shown that the general expansion of the eighteenth century meant not only a growth in production but also an increase in real income per capita, measured in particular by the upward movement of real wages. It was only after 1780 that the Catalan expansion was threatened or blocked: prices then outstripped the nominal income from the land.

Overall, the eighteenth century in Spain was a prosperous period of long-term growth. There were certain areas of conflict: between the interests of those encouraging the farmers to produce cereals and those who wanted them to increase their wool output. Spain, and especially Castille, produced fine wool which was in great demand on the markets of northern Europe where it satisfied the needs of an expanding textile industry. In Estramadure, for example, the *Mesta*, a famous organization of sheep owners, was very powerful throughout the eighteenth century. It encouraged transhumance, which created serious problems for the grain-producing farmers.

Spain was not the only place in the world to experience a period of expansion in the eighteenth century. It had an even more vigorous counterpart in the sharp increase in the production of subsistence crops in Latin America.[24] In Mexico expansion, which had begun in 1670, was still going on in 1800 or even later, thanks to the ease with which land could be taken into cultivation and to the increase in population which occurred at the same time. These two factors were clearly more important in the New World than in Europe.

Comparative study of trends

I have two general points to make about the expansion in Spain in the eighteenth century:

(a) it developed over a long period, since it began to be evident from 1670 on. It also does not appear to have slowed down or stopped during the crisis years 1690–1715 – as happened in France and Portugal for example. The expansion in Spain certainly showed a few signs of losing momentum from the middle of the eighteenth century; it did, however, revive between the 1750s and the 1780s in different parts of the country, especially in the more dynamic areas like Catalonia. Of course, what was taking place in Spain was part of a general cycle of growth in eighteenth-century Europe; there was even what may be called a world expansion. The two Americas, North and South, and China also showed signs of a vigorous economic and demographic increase during this period.

(b) The expansion in Spain (unlike England) did not lead to 'a great leap forward' towards new forms of industrialization (though there were a few important developments in traditional industries in the Iberian peninsula at this period). Spanish wool production increased and cloth production was industrialized, though only further north, in France and England. The same applies to silk: it was produced in Italy but woven in Lyons.

Were the trends very different in Portugal? The Portuguese expansion in the eighteenth century, as calculated from the tithes and from the grain yields, seems to have reached a peak around 1740–67. After this there were certain signs of decline. However, the benefits of the moderate expansion which Portugal was experiencing at this period were often capitalized elsewhere; England was one country that profited from this. The statistics for Portugal are fairly detailed, thanks to the research done on the tithes by de Oliveira. The tithe reached a first peak during the 1680s, giving a considerable boost to the fortunes of the Catholic, baroque Church of Portugal. This was followed by a period of severe crisis between 1683 and 1713, after

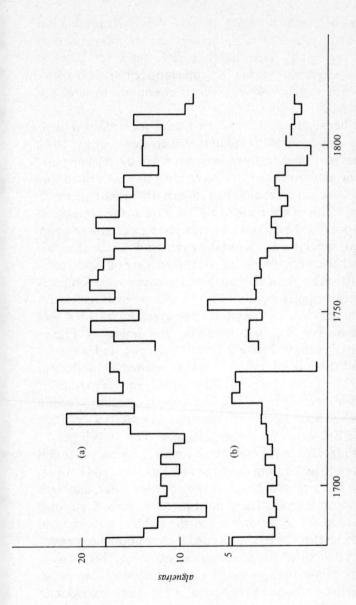

12. Grain tithes and income from land belonging to the Abbey of Tibaes, Portugal, 1683–1813 (Derived from data made available by A. de Oliveira)

(a) = tithes (maslin) (b) = harvests from land under direct exploitation by the abbey 1 *algueira* = 14–18 litres

algueiras

which there was a return to high levels of production from 1715 until 1761. In the best decade, from 1740 to 1749, the results were slightly better (index 100) than in the best decade of the seventeenth century (1680–9: index 87). After 1767 the situation appears to have deteriorated.[25]

It is beyond dispute that there was an increase in agricultural production in France in the eighteenth century. How are we to calculate this? We can start by rejecting the extreme views of Morineau, according to which there was no increase in production or productivity in the eighteenth century. This is not reasonable. As long as the population of France did not exceed – or only just exceeded – 20 or 21 million inhabitants, between 1320 and 1720 approximately, the agricultural ecosystem in general and cereal production in particular oscillated between fixed limits, as Morineau rightly points out. On this point I agree with him. In the eighteenth century, however, the situation was different. For the first time the population of France increased sharply between 1715 and 1789 and went far beyond the old 20 million level. It reached 27 million in 1789. These extra mouths had to be fed, and, in particular, fed with their 'daily bread'. The level of cereal production which had been achieved in the time of Louis XIV – or Philippe le Bel – was no longer adequate. The French people were in fact fed in the eighteenth century: famines were still a serious threat during the reign of Louis XIV (1661, 1694, 1709), but after this last date they became rarer, and even more so after 1740. There must therefore have been some increase in cereal production in the eighteenth century in France, so that the level exceeded the traditional ceilings of the fourteenth to the seventeenth centuries. This increase need not have been proportional to the increase in population. In fact it must have been a little lower – a good indication of this is the fact that in France, as in England, the price of wheat calculated in grammes of silver rose regularly and steadily from 1734: the increase in demand was thus greater than the increase in supply. In any case, there did not have to be an exact balance: the construction of roads and barns meant that grains could be stored and transported to areas that were temporarily short. During the reign of Louis XIV dreadful famines were commonplace; in the reigns of Louis XV and Louis XVI, at least after 1740, they no longer occurred.

It may be useful to estimate the increase in the cereal product in France in the eighteenth century. In England it increased by 34.5% between 1700 and 1790, while the population increased by 41.5%.[26] If the increase in France was similar in scale, it could have been 23% between 1700 and 1789, when the population increased by 28%. It seems plausible to suggest that the production of cereals in France increased by at least 20% between 1700 and 1789. In any case, it cannot be denied that there was a positive trend.

It should be pointed out in passing that the first figure suggested by Toutain for the increase in the agricultural product, and more precisely in the cereal product, in France in the eighteenth century was too high. It was flattering for French pride: it was comparable to the English successes in the eighteenth century. Toutain suggested that the total agricultural product increased by 60% in real terms between 1700 and 1789 and that the cereal product by itself increased by 43% (the average of three possible estimates).[27] In fact this optimistic assessment was based on the guesswork of Gregory King, which was to the point for England but quite inadequate for France.[28] I repeat that the increase in the cereal product in France may have been about 20% or a little more. The increase in the general agricultural product, including wine and animal products etc., was probably greater; in the eighteenth century in France there had in fact been a diversification in agricultural production which favoured non-cereal products, especially stockraising. As far as the overall agricultural product is concerned, it is at the moment not possible to verify an increase of 30% between 1710 and 1789, but this is certainly a more reasonable estimate than Toutain's 60%. In any case, a figure of around 40% would appear to be beyond the maximum. There is, however, one problem if we are to compare the 1700s with the 1780s: in France, at least, the severe depression at the end of Louis XIV's reign ran into the early eighteenth century. The result is to exaggerate the eighteenth century expansion by measuring it from a point which is decidedly too low.

Another approach seems to me more realistic: we should ask ourselves whether the ceiling of agricultural production in France in the eighteenth century – that of the 1780s – was in fact higher than the ceiling of the seventeenth century – that of the relatively good period of Colbert's ministry. It is very probable that the ceiling of the 1780s was higher than that of the years 1660–80: since the population of France scarcely exceeded, if it indeed reached, 20 million inhabitants in Colbert's time, whereas, I repeat, it reached 27 million during the 1780s. We can assume, then, that the agricultural product in general, and the cereal product in particular, increased between these two dates; there was, in short, an absolute increase in food production between these two decades a century apart, and this made it possible to feed the extra 7 million population. This suggestion seems all the more likely since famines disappeared during the period 1740–89.

As it happens, real life did conform to this theory. It is enough to look at the curves of the tithe and rents (expressed in real terms). As early as 1971 Dupâquier showed me certain data on agriculture in the Vexin.[29] This was a fairly dynamic region: the Paris market provided a positive stimulus, the soil was fertile and agriculture was organized on semi-capitalist lines. The eighteenth-century expansion had in any case been marked in the Paris region: rents there rose by 30% in real terms between 1740 and 1780.[30] It is therefore not surprising that Dupâquier's data on the Vexin indicate that the cereal tithe increased by 23.2% in *real* terms between the Colbert years (1660–85) and the end of the *ancien régime* (1778–88). There was a distinct increase in wealth among the better-off rural groups around Paris between the Colbert period and Louis XVI's reign. This is clearly demonstrated by the wills made in these two periods: in the eighteenth century the yeomen owned a greater variety and quantity of material goods, and their quality and value had also increased.[31] The same applies to inventories post mortem deposited with notaries in Languedoc from the seventeenth to the eighteenth centuries.[32]

We must not, of course, adopt Pangloss' naïve opinion that everything was for the best in the best of worlds in the countryside around Paris at this period. Cereal production increased; but in many cases the population increased more rapidly, especially after 1760. This was true, for example, in the little rural area of Thimerais, near Paris: there, cereal production did increase but the increase in population outstripped it between 1720 and 1790. This was bound to lead to problems, even allowing for the fact that the level of the cereal product in the 1780s was very probably higher than that achieved in Colbert's time.

It may be useful to give a rapid summary of Derouet's thesis on this problem in the Thimerais.[33] This enables us to put into perspective the undeniable increases in production which took place between the Colbert and the Necker eras. This eighteenth-century expansion lagged behind the increase in population: this imposed certain constraints; the Thimerais and other rural societies of the period had to develop regulating mechanisms; the needs and levels of the population had to be adjusted according to the food available. This was achieved by raising the age of marriage, especially for women and especially amongst agricultural workers, who were the social groups most at risk in periods when the real per capita income declined. Another regulation mechanism was a decline in fertility, noticeable in the Thimerais after 1760. This restriction of births can be explained by the practice of *coïtus interruptus*, especially in the period 1760–80 when the population was more educated than in the past. Derouet, however, is sceptical about this: he believes that the decline in fertility after 1760, measured by the lengthening of the birth intervals, was often due to natural causes, such as miscarriages. Whether the birth rate was voluntarily or involuntarily controlled, it was in any case affected by increased poverty which weakened the lower strata of society and made them more susceptible to disease. As a result, after 1760 there was in this region a considerable increase in the percentage of babies who died within 24 hours of birth: this supports the hypothesis of an increase in the number of miscarriages.

The fact that the birth rate dropped, whatever the reason, is significant from a Malthusian point of view; it mainly affected the poorest sector of society, in other words the agricultural labourers rather than the yeomen farmers.

The problems pinpointed by Malthus can also be observed in another area in the Thimerais in the eighteenth century: cereal production did not increase as quickly as the population; this created a classic situation in which the mortality rate amongst the labourers rose after 1765 compared with that of the yeomen farmers who were distinctly better off. This increase in mortality was particularly pronounced amongst the children of agricultural labourers between the ages of one and fifteen.

The death rate is not the only factor to be considered: there was also a trend towards downward social mobility, owing to this process of impoverishment and to the opening of the Malthusian scissors which widened the gap between population and production. The sons of yeomen farmers became agricultural labourers; they were confined to this lower stratum for a long time – sometimes their whole lives. This meant that the percentage of labourers in rural society noticeably increased after 1760.

During the years 1730–60, when the long-term upward trend was showing only positive tendencies, the predominant social group in the Thimerais was the 'lower middle' class, made up of people known as *sossons*, who cultivated small or medium-sized farms; they were not crushed by poverty. After 1760 the effect of the 'centrifugal force' became more obvious. The increase in population resulted in a higher percentage of labourers in the community, whereas at the other end of the social scale the wealthy farmers became more numerous and more important. The intermediate group, or lower middle class of *sossons*, tended to be crushed between these two extremes.

When we speak, then, of an increase in production, and especially in cereal production in France in the eighteenth century, we must not forget the following two aspects of the problem.

(1) There was an undeniable increase between 1700 and 1789, and an even more significant one between the 1680s and the 1780s; it enriched certain sectors of the rural population.

(2) This increase in production could not altogether keep pace with the increase in population; this discrepancy led, according to Malthusian principles, to mechanisms like late marriages, an increase in the death rate among the poor, and a reduction in the birth rate as a result of either contraception or pathological factors.

Once we have these clarifications it seems to me that we are in a better position to take an overall look at the expansion of agricultural production in France in the eighteenth century. I have mentioned the fact that in the Paris Basin this increase did not merely mean that the levels of the 1780s were higher than those of 1700; they were also distinctly higher than the maximum ceilings which had been achieved in the 'good' Colbert years. This is also true for the Cambrésis and for other areas in the extreme north of France: in these regions the tithe curve for the Louis XVI period is distinctly higher than for the Colbert era. I should reiterate, however, that at this Colbert period in the Cambrésis the levels of cereal production, excluding other

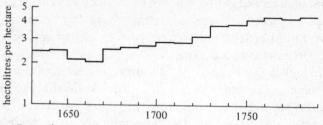

13. Rates of rents paid in wheat in the vicinity of Caen, Normandy, 1630–1790 (derived from data made available by J. M. Pavard)

animal or vegetable products, were only as high as those which had been achieved before the Black Death.

The statistics for Normandy have been studied by Garnier, Pavard, Perrot and other researchers, who have looked at tithes in kind and at tithes and rents calculated in real terms. All the evidence indicates that the increases in the tithes and rents in Normandy in the eighteenth century were not merely achieved by 'turning the screw' on the peasants, but did in fact reflect an increase in the gross agricultural product itself, to well above the levels of the seventeenth century. In the north of the Cotentin, a 'frontier' area where the forests were gradually destroyed or cleared in the period, the seventeenth century, from Louis XIII on, fared better than the sixteenth. And in turn, the eighteenth century, after 1730, did better than even the best levels of the seventeenth century. In the Bocage of Normandy, the sixteenth-century ceilings had been equalled but not exceeded during the seventeenth century. They were definitively exceeded in the eighteenth century, when the production of buckwheat spread widely through these woodlands, as in Brittany. The Caen plain had an advanced system of agriculture, by French if not by English standards. It had large farms supplying the urban market in Caen. In this area too the eighteenth century was a period of expansion: the levels of production which had been reached in the seventeenth century doubled around 1770, whereas in the Cotentin – which was certainly less fertile and less urbanized – expansion over this same period was only 60–62%. This increase in the gross product in the Caen plain benefited the local farmers. In real terms, the rents paid by the farmer to the landowner increased by only 50 to 60% over the same period; this left the farmers with a larger surplus since their output had doubled.[34] It was not only cereal production that increased in the region around Caen; stockbreeding did too.[35] This is indicated by the rents which were obtained for meadow land in Lower Normandy. In real terms, the rent for grazing land rose by 52.9% between 1730 and 1790.[36]

The area around Lisieux was less impressive than that around Caen: the product of the cereal tithe rose by only 14% in real terms in the 1770s compared with the highest ceilings it had reached in the time of Louis XIII or of Colbert.

The interesting case of the Pays d'Auge deserves a brief mention.[37] In this area fields previously used for cereal crops continued to be converted into grazing land for cattle into the eighteenth century: this was in order to satisfy the increased demand for meat products from the Paris market. Although this practice was by definition unfavourable to cereal production, the grain tithe did not fall much further in the Pays d'Auge in the eighteenth century.[38] This was because of the use of fertilizers: stockbreeding was expanding, and the manure obtained tended to increase the grain yields and so may have compensated for the loss of acreage.

On the whole, there was a remarkable expansion in Normandy in the eighteenth century, especially if one compares it with the stagnation of agriculture in neighbouring Brittany. The Norman performance is all the more interesting in that it took place at a time when the population was increasing fairly slowly. According to Pierre Chaunu, the population of Normandy increased by only 10% (9.7% to be precise) during the eighteenth century.[39] The cereal product rose by 49% in the same period (this is the average for the four zones of Normandy for which we have data, three of which – Caen, the Lieuvin and the Cotentin – were expanding). From this, then, we can see that the increase in the cereal product per capita in Normandy was 36% from the seventeenth century to the end of the eighteenth. It is in this context that we should understand the Norman farmers' Malthusian motto 'not more than one calf in the meadow'. Not more than one male child to inherit the family farm... This was quite enough to eradicate famine and raise the standard of living, that of the countryside included. The rural economy of Normandy was certainly one of the most dynamic in France at this period, but it was not the only one in the world. Even in the south of France there were regions where agriculture expanded between the Colbert and the Necker periods; without this economic expansion, the demographic increase of the eighteenth century would have generated spectacular famines which we know did not actually take place.

Let us look, for example, at the estates of the Knights of St John in the Aquitaine Basin. The curves for the income of these estates, adjusted according to prices in Toulouse, is very revealing (see Figure 14). They show a distinct increase around 1715–20 as they emerge from the depths of the end of Louis XIV's reign; this upward trend continued for the first twenty years of Louis XV's reign, which were the good years of Cardinal Fleury's ministry. By 1736 the high levels of the Colbert period were within 10% of being recovered. The expansion then continued; in the second half of the eighteenth century the records of the Colbert period were surpassed. The upper limit to growth which had lasted so long was exceeded at last. In four regions, Toulouse, the mid-Garonne, the foothills of the Pyrenees and the area around Bordeaux, the level of 1789 was on average 18.5% higher than that of the years around 1678, even though the latter was a typically high level from the Colbert period.[40] The tithes for Toulouse, which have been studied by Frêche, had been disturbed by active or

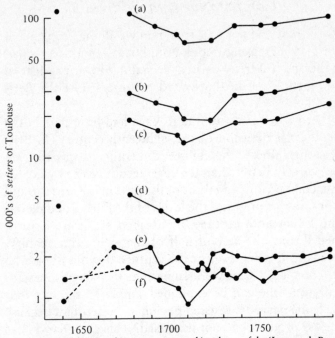

14. Global and regional income, expressed in wheat, of the 'Langue de Provence' (estates of the Knights of St John), 1640–1790 (derived from data made available by G. Gangneux)

(a) = Langue de Provence   (b) = Toulouse (total)   (c) = mid-Garonne
(d) = Pre-Pyrenees   (e) = Perigord   (f) = Bordelais

passive resistance on the part of those liable to pay them.[41] The tithes of this period were thus not a very precise means of calculating growth, especially in certain southern areas. The estates of the Knights of St John are more reliable, whether one looks at the tithe or at the rents received by the Order. Elsewhere, Gangneux uses certain qualitative data which also indicate expansion. These data concern the development of vines, mulberries and olives and of terraced cultivation on hillsides. There is also evidence of some land clearance and certain innovations in agronomy. These data confirm the modest but undeniable upward trend in the south in the eighteenth century: thanks to Gangneux this is now solidly documented with statistics. This moderate upward trend did not, it is true, remove all the problems of feeding an increasing population, but it cannot be denied that the upward trend existed, even if it does not appear to have reached certain backward provinces, like the Perigord.[42]

Other regions also appear to have had little part in the agricultural expansion of the eighteenth century. In Brittany, for example, the eighteenth century seems to have done scarcely better than the seventeenth century, according to Tim Le Goff's analysis of the tithe in the area around Vannes. In this province the levels of the fairly good period of the seventeenth century (the Colbert era) were at most gained during the second half of the eighteenth century, whereas in the first half of the century they had not even been equalled.[43] Can we assume that this sluggishness of the Breton tithe can be explained simply by the fact that there some peasants resisted paying it, rather than because the gross product had not increased? This explanation has some force. In 1789 the Breton peasants, some of whom were later to become royalists and counter-revolutionaries, publicly declared themselves against their feudal lords and against the tithe; they even attacked a few châteaux. All the same, there probably was a certain stagnation in real terms in agriculture in Brittany in the eighteenth century, even if this was simply the result of the low growth rate of the population in the province at this period. At the end of the seventeenth century Brittany had around 2 million inhabitants, in 1790 there were 2,200,000. This represented an increase of only 10%: very much below the increase for France as a whole, which was 28%. Agricultural expansion in Brittany was not stimulated by a sharp increase in population. This would explain the stagnation of the regional tithe, which was perhaps further reduced by tithe 'strikes'. It will be objected that I am contradicting myself; in Normandy I pointed out that there was simultaneously a *slow* increase in the population (10%) and a remarkable expansion in the agricultural product (49% for cereals). In Brit-

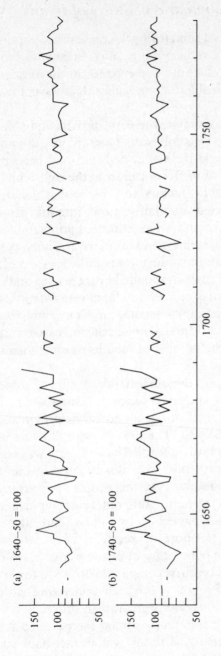

15. Grain tithes in the vicinity of Vannes, Brittany, 1628–1785 (Le Goff)

tany there was a similar slow increase in the population (by only 10% in a century); but, in contrast with Normandy, the cereal product did not expand: in the 1780s the tithe levels were hardly, if at all, higher than those for the years 1660–80.

Let us try to compare these two provinces: in Normandy, as Chaunu and his followers have shown, the population was already relatively educated and had been practising certain forms of birth control from the eighteenth century: this was one of the factors (together with a high death rate) which explained the fairly slow rate of demographic growth in Normandy. This educated population consisted of landowners, farmers and ordinary peasants; they felt the pressures of the expanding food markets, especially around Paris. These farmers responded by increasing and diversifying agricultural production so far as cereals, cattle etc. were concerned. Per capita income in Normandy rose during this period, since the economic cake increased considerably in size while the number of mouths to eat it increased very little.

In Brittany, on the other hand, in spite of some notable successes in the maritime sector at Nantes, Saint-Malo and some smaller ports, the economy of the province remained generally backward. The masses were illiterate and there was very little birth control. The birth rate was very high.[44] So was the death rate. Was this because of the desperate lack of hygiene amongst the people of Brittany at this period? They certainly suffered severe epidemics. Contagious diseases passed on by sailors (and others) spread inland from the port of Brest.[45] These various factors meant that the population of Brittany rose by only 10% in the eighteenth century, compared with 28% for France as a whole; they also indicate that the underlying causes of this demographic increase were rather different from those underlying the apparently similar increase (10% again) in nearby Normandy. Brittany was in fact backward, Normandy relatively advanced.

The economic behaviour of the respective population of the two provinces also reflects this contrast between the lack of development and relative progressiveness. The Normans responded to the pressures of the market: they increased and diversified the agricultural product. The Bretons were less enterprising and less flexible. They may, however, be excused: the expanding Paris market was further away from them than from Normandy. In Brittany, then, the agricultural product did not increase much, at least as far as cereals were concerned. Any increase that did take place merely reflected the slight increase in the local population. What is more, rents increased in Brittany in the eighteenth century, and apparently at a faster rate than production. The situation here was thus quite unlike that in Normandy, where the farmers gained relative to the landowners in the eighteenth century and where real per capita income was expanding; the Breton peasants of the Vannetais were fleeced more and more severely by the landowners in this period, since rents increased while the cereal product did not.

If one looks at the curves, Anjou, Maine and Poitou appear to have experienced a period of stagnation or low growth in the agricultural product similar to that in Brittany. However, we must be aware of the possibility that the tithe and even rents in these provinces may have been the object of fraud. This fraud may flatten the local curves for the eighteenth century.[46]

In Savoy, there was an instance of real agricultural growth, even if our measuring instruments (in this case, the tithe) have been made unusable by the very people liable to pay it. The tithe in Savoy indicates that after 1715–20 the crisis of the end of Louis XIV's reign had come to an end. Louis XIV, of course, did not have any royal (or ducal) power over Savoy at this period, but, as a result of the wars, a period of crisis contemporary with that in France tended to spread into countries like Savoy and even Portugal at this time. These countries were in fact directly affected by the wars in which their powerful neighbour, France, was engaged.

In Savoy, then, the crisis at the end of Louis XIV's reign came to an end after 1715; after this came a period of recovery. However, if one follows the tithe figures one has the impression that the levels of agricultural production in Savoy in the 1780s are scarcely any higher than those which had been recorded in the 1680s, reinforcing the theory that the agricultural product remained stagnant in France during the *ancien régime*. But once again, this theory would make it difficult to account for a number of facts. For the population of Savoy increased considerably during the eighteenth century – by more than 25%, from 320,000 inhabitants to 400,000. Since famines had more or less died out in Savoy at this period and since transport facilities had not improved much in this mountainous region, the historian has little choice but to admit that there *was* agricultural expansion in Savoy in the eighteenth century. Jean Nicolas, the distinguished historian of Savoy, looks beyond the evidence from the tithe, which has been shown to be inadequate and even irrelevant in this case. By using other sources, Nicolas shows that in this area there was already a fairly remarkable expansion in the cultivation of maize and of potatoes in the eighteenth century. Potatoes were grown in Savoy from 1742 on; in the district of Faucigny, after a period of expansion, potatoes accounted for 25% of agricultural production in 1789. This is how they solved the problem of adapting agricultural production to an increasing population in this area. Of course, this does not mean that the peasants of Savoy lived like princes during the 1780s. In fact, many of them developed goitres as a result of certain mineral deficiencies in the local water; in a large valley like Maurienne there was not a single doctor at the end of the *ancien régime*! Just folk healers, or quacks...

If the agricultural expansion in Savoy in the eighteenth century cannot be calculated from the tithe, at least it is reflected in certain data relating to the cereal product. Even if the tithe figures are misleading, the data relative to taxes on the import and consumption of wheat at Annecy indicate that there was a large quantity of wheat taxed at this market at the end of the sixteenth century which corresponded to the high levels of grain production in neighbouring northern Italy. After this came a period of crisis in the seventeenth century: 30 measures or scoops of wheat were taxed, then 25 scoops around 1690. During the eighteenth century, though, there was an expansion: 40 scoops around 1705–40, and finally 80 to 90 scoops between 1750 and 1780 – a level which exceeded the previous records (those of the sixteenth century). It was probably the influence of the growing urban markets that stimulated cereal production in the surrounding countryside. There was also an increase in the number of head of cattle in Savoy in the eighteenth century: the number of cows, oxen and calves increased by 21% between 1708 and 1788. What is more, the individual weight of these animals rose by 19.5% between 1730 and 1788; the real growth of cattle in Savoy in the eighteenth century was thus close to 44.6%.[47]

A. Molinier has studied the data for the Vivarais in his recent thesis.[48] This indicates that the agriculture of the mountainous regions of south-east France – like that of Savoy – was able to support the increase in population. Despite this demographic increase, the inhabitants were able to maintain their calorie level, notably by the increasing consumption of chestnuts. The level of calories per head was low in the Vivarais; but at least it remained stable throughout the eighteenth century.

In Switzerland the cereal product scarcely increased, despite a slight upturn in the first half of the eighteenth century. But agriculture became more specialized: as Van der Wee points out, this raised the level of productivity; it meant that the best possible returns could be obtained from soils of different qualities.[49] For example, in those areas of Switzerland where there was already some wine production this was increased at the expense of wheat production. This was the opposite process to that which had occurred in Switzerland in the sixteenth century: then, straightforward subsistence foods, like grain, had been the first concern of the farmers.

In any case, the fact that cereal production appears to have stagnated in Switzerland was not necessarily a bad sign: in the towns the consumption of wheat or bread did decrease (unlike the situation in Annecy in Savoy); on the other hand, the consumption of meat per capita increased in Geneva: it rose from 60 kg per inhabitant at the beginning of the eighteenth century to 75 kg at the end.[50] Meat was very cheap in this area: pound per pound, it cost only 67% more than bread! There was probably more land given over to grazing, especially at high altitudes.[51] During this period fewer fields were left fallow; there was an increase in the cultivation of leguminous vegetables and potatoes (the latter especially after 1790). The dangerous fluctuations in the yield from certain cereals tended to even out, especially in the case of spelt. Thus the fact that the tithe product remained stable does not necessarily mean there was no possible increase in population.

At the end of this examination of the tithe and related problems in the eighteenth century, it appears that there was on the whole a general, if unequal, increase in agricultural production throughout Western Europe and to a certain extent in Central Europe, with the possible exception of Hungary. This increase in agricultural production in general, and specifically in cereal production, did not always result in an increase in the food available per head, though this was sometimes the case, for example in Normandy. There is no doubt, however, that the overall volume increased; in many cases it clearly exceeded the previous records of the pre-plague fourteenth century. This was especially important in the case of cereals, since the levels of grain production had been particularly high in the years 1320–40. There was also an unprecedented increase in livestock during the eighteenth century. However, these statements are not universally valid: we have seen how in the eighteenth century the levels of non-cereal products in the Cambrésis did exceed the pre-plague levels, but the levels of cereal production in the time of Louis XVI only equalled those which had been reached three and a half centuries earlier during the reign of Philippe le Bel. All the same, the establishment in the eighteenth century of these new records, which exceeded those of the early fourteenth century, was largely the result of increases in the cereal product as well as of a diversification of agricultural production to include other vegetable crops and livestock.

There is no call for Panglossian optimism. The truth of Malthus' and Ricardo's pessimistic theories is clearly reflected in the facts, even before these two thinkers were writing. Even in England at the beginning of the industrial revolution the problem pointed out by Malthus was apparent. The increase in grain prices which took place in Great Britain during the second half of the eighteenth century does seem to show that here, too, the increase in the agricultural product did not keep pace with the increase in population. This applied even more to France: according to a detailed study, in the Paris Basin the widening gap between population and income influenced the birth, marriage and death rates, with death, unfortunately, in the lead. Finally, the obstacles that according to Malthus restricted demographic growth – obstacles which derived from the lack of flexibility in the production of foodstuffs for the market – were probably even more effective in Mediterranean countries like Spain and Italy; there, the expansion in agriculture which was a feature of the eighteenth century tended to slow down, and sometimes stopped altogether, from 1750–60.

It was only really in the nineteenth century that the Malthusian problem was resolved – when, thanks to different forms of progress, especially technological – production was able to keep pace with, or even keep ahead of, population growth instead of struggling painfully behind.

Notes

1. The tithe: an old source for new research

1 Pierre Goubert, *Beauvais et le Beauvaisis de 1600 à 1730*, Paris, 1960. Abridged edition: *Cent mille provinciaux au XVIIe siècle*, Paris, 1968.

2 Title of a review-article by E. Le Roy Ladurie in *Etudes Rurales* 13–14 (1964).

3 R. Baehrel, *Une croissance. La Basse-Provence rurale (fin du XVIe siècle – 1789)*, Paris, 1961.

4 English ed., Urbana, Ill., 1974. Originally published in French as *Les paysans de Languedoc*, Paris, 1966; 2nd ed., 1974; abridged ed. (same title), 1969.

5 J. Goy and E. Le Roy Ladurie (eds.), *Les fluctuations du produit de la dîme. Conjoncture décimale et domaniale de la fin du Moyen-Age au XVIIIe siècle*, Paris, 1972.

6 See Chapter 3 for a discussion of methodological questions.

7 M. Morineau, *Les faux-semblants d'un démarrage économique: agriculture et démographie en France au XVIIIe siècle*, Paris, 1970. See also his article 'Y-a-t-il eu une révolution agricole en France au XVIIIe siècle?' in *Revue Historique* (April–June 1968).

8 P. Deyon, *Contribution a l'étude des revenus fonciers en Picardie. Les fermages de l'Hôtel-Dieu d'Amiens et leurs variations de 1515 à 1789*, Lille, no date.

9 'La mesure de la production agricole sous l'Ancien Régime', *Annales E.S.C.* 4 (1964).

10 *16. Szazadi Dezsmajegyzekek* (Sixteenth-century Tithe Registers), Budapest, 1960; a vast collection of tithe series amounting to over 1,000 pages. Z. Kirilly and I. -N. Kiss, 'Production de céréales et exploitations paysannes en Hongrie aux XVIe-XVIIe siècles', *Annales E.S.C.* 6 (1968).

11 'La Armuña y su evolución economica', *Estudios geograficos* 58 and 59.

12 See especially Gonzalo Anes and Jean-Paul Le Flem, 'La crisis del siglo XVII. Producción agricolo, precios e ingresos en tierras de Segovia', *Moneda y Credito* 93 (1961), and G. Anes, *Las crisis agrarias en la España moderna*, Madrid, 1970. For an exhaustive bibliography of work on Spain, see Guy Lemeunier, *La part de*

Dieu, Mélanges de la Casa de Velasquez XI, Madrid, 1975, and the report to the Edinburgh Congress by Anes and Angel Garcia Sanz (cf. p. 7).

13 *Actas de las jornadas de metodologia aplicada de las ciencias históricas, ponencias y comunicaciones* vol. III. 4a, Vigo, 1975. See especially E. Labrousse, 'Aspects d'un bilan méthodologique et critique de l'histoire conjoncturelle' and the contributions of B. Barreiro Maccon, A. Garcia Sanz, A. Eiras Roel, L. M. Bilbao and E. Fernandez de Pinedo for the regions of Xallas, Segovia, Galicia and the Alava plain.

14 Section A3, 'Prestations paysannes, dîmes et mouvements de la production agricole dans les sociétés pré-industrielles'. This immense conference was made possible through the assistance of the Ministère des Universités, the Ministère des Affaires Etrangères, the Collège de France and the EHESS.

15 See Appendix (p. 9).

16 M. Carmagnani, 'La producción agro pacuaria chilena (1680–1830)', *Cahiers des Amériques Latines* 3 (1969), and *Les mécanismes de la vie économique dans une société coloniale: le Chili (1680–1830)*, Paris, 1973.

17 University Press, Edinburgh, 1978.

18 This paper has also been published in a revised version in E. Le Roy Ladurie and J. Goy, 'La dîme et le reste XIVe–XVIIIe siècles', *Revue Historique* 527 (July–Sept. 1973), 123–42.

19 This paper was actually published in the second volume of the *Proceedings* (pp. 541–50).

20 Louvain, 1978. The volume contains the following:
(a) The introductory report by Van der Wee entitled 'The Agricultural Development of the Low Countries as revealed by the Tithe and Rent Statistics, 1250–1800'.
(b) Four papers given at the Paris conference.
M.-P. Gutman, 'War, the Tithe and Agricultural Production: the Meuse Basin North of Liège, 1661–1740'.
M.-J. Tits-Dieuaide, 'Cereal Yields around Louvain, 1404–1729'.
E. Van Cauwenberghe and H. Van der Wee, 'Productivity, Evolution of Rents and Farm Size in the Southern Netherlands Agriculture from the Fourteenth to the Seventeenth Century'.
A.-M. Van der Woude, 'The Long-term Movement of Rent for Pasture Land in North Holland and the Problem of Profitability in Agriculture (1570–1800)'.
(c) Five other contributions:
F. Daelemans, 'Tithe Revenues in Rural South-West Brabant, Fifteenth to Eighteenth Centuries'.
F. De Wever, 'Rents and Selling Prices of Land at Zele, Sixteenth to Eighteenth Centuries'.
J. C. G. M. Jansen, 'Tithes and the Productivity of Land in the South of Limburg, 1348–1790'.
M.-J. Tits-Dieuaide, 'Peasant Dues in Brabant. The Example of the

Meldert Farm near Tirlemont (1380–1787)'.

C. Vandenbroecke and W. Verderpijpen, 'The Problem of the "Agricultural Revolution" in Flanders and in Belgium: Myth or Reality?'

21 A. Verhulst and C. Vandenbroecke (eds.), *Landbouwproduktiviteit in Vlaanderen en Brabant 14de – 18de eeuw.*, Studia Historica Gandensia 223 (1979).

22 *La Jurisdicción de Xallas a lo largo del siglo XVIII. Poblacion, sociedad y economica*, Santiago, 1973.

23 *Diezmos y tributos del clero de Granada*, Granada, 1974.

24 E. F. Pinedo, *Crecimiento economico y transformaciones sociales del Pais Vasco, 1150–1850*, Madrid, 1974.

25 *Desarollo y crisis del Antiguo Regimen en Castilla la Vieja. Economia y sociedad en tierras de Segovia, 1550–1814*, Madrid, 1977.

26 *Diezmo ecclasiastico y produccion de cereales en el reino de Sevilla, (1408–1503)*, Seville, 1979.

2. The tithe in France and elsewhere

1 See on this subject the most important works from a vast bibliography:
P. Gagnol, *La dîme ecclésiastique en France*, Paris, 1911.
H. Marion, *La dîme ecclésiastique en France au XVIIIe siècle*, Paris, 1912.
P. Viard, *Histoire de la dîme ecclésiastique en France au XVIIe siècle*, Paris, 1914.

2 It sometimes happened that the collection of certain long-established tithes became increasingly difficult, so that more emphasis was placed on the exceptional tithes. On the other hand, in certain regions in the eighteenth century, new crops were exempt from the tithe.

3 The tithe could be 'enfeoffed', in other words, held as a fief by a layman who had either taken it or bought it. Merchants and, still more often, local squires owned tithes in the eighteenth century.

4 J. Goy and A. L. Head-Koenig, 'Une expérience. Les revenus décimaux en France méditerranéenne, XVIe–XVIIIe siècles', *Etudes Rurales* 36 (1969); Goy and Le Roy Ladurie (1972).

5 H. Neveux, *Les grains du Cambrésis (fin du XIVe-début du XVIIe siècles). Vie et déclin d'une structure économique*, Paris, 1980.

6 G. Frêche, *Toulouse et la région Midi-Pyrénées au Siècle des Lumières, vers 1670–1789*, Paris, 1974.

7 G. Bois, *Crise du féodalisme. Economie rurale et démographie en Normandie orientale au début du XVIe siècle*, Paris, 1976.

8 J. Nicolas, *La Savoie au XVIIIe siècle. Noblesse et bourgeoisie*, Paris, 1978.

9 Goy and Le Roy Ladurie (1972); see the Appendix to Chapter 1.

10 See for example A. Poitrineau, *La vie rurale en Basse-Auvergne au XVIIIe siècle (1726–1789)*, Paris, 1965, and Guy Cabourdin,

Terre et hommes en Lorraine, 1550–1635, Toulois et Comté de Vaudémont, Nancy, 1977.

11 The Paris conference previously mentioned. The papers are to be published as the *Actes du Colloque préparatoire* (forthcoming); the list of contents is set out as the Appendix to Chapter 1, p. 9.

12 For this material, see L. Makkai's paper at the Edinburgh Congress, *Proceedings* 1, and the sections on Hungary in the *Actes du Colloque préparatoire* (forthcoming).

13 'Tithes and Agricultural Production in Modern Spain', *Proceedings* 2, pp. 541ff.

14 Paper by Claude Morin in *Actes du Colloque préparatoire* (forthcoming).

15 B. Anatra, 'Cenni sulla produzione cerealicola nella Sardegna barocca', *Actes du Colloque préparatoire* (forthcoming). M. A. Visceglia, 'Rente féodale et agriculture dans Les Pouilles à l'époque moderne (XVIe-XVIIIe siècles)', *Actes du Colloque préparatoire* (forthcoming).

16 M. Aymard and G. L. Basini, 'Production et productivité agricoles en Italie (XVIe–XVIIIe siècles)', *Proceedings* 1, pp. 137ff.

17 A. L. Head-Koenig, 'La mesure de la production et des rendements céréaliers en Allemagne et en Suisse à l'époque moderne', *Proceedings* 1, pp. 153ff.
See also: A. L. Head-Koenig and B. Veyrassat-Herren, 'Les revenus décimaux à Genève de 1540 à 1783', in J. Goy and E. Le Roy Ladurie (1972) and 'La production agricole du Plateau Suisse aux XVIIe et XVIIIe siècle', *Revue Suisse d'Histoire* 20 (1970). T. Pfister, 'Agrarkonjunktur und Wiherungsverlouf im westlichen Schweizen Mittelland 1755–1797', *Geographica Bernensia* G.2 (1975).

18 Jerzy Topolski and Andrzej Wyczanski, 'Les fluctuations de la production agricole en Pologne aux XVIe–XVIIIe siècles', *Actes du Colloque préparatoire* (forthcoming).

19 'A Parallel Study of Agricultural Production and of the Feudal Duties of Peasantry in Estonia (16th–19th centuries)', *Actes du Colloque préparatoire* (forthcoming).

20 Contribution by N. E. Nossov made at the Edinburgh Congress: 'A propos du problème de la "corvée" paysanne et du servage en Russie'.

21 See Goy and Le Roy Ladurie (1972); *Proceedings* vols. 1 and 2, and *Actes du Colloque préparatoire* (forthcoming).

22 See A. L. Head-Koenig, 'Les fluctuations des rendements et du produit décimal dans quelques régions du Plateau Suisse du XVIe au XVIIIe', *Actes du Colloque préparatoire* (forthcoming).

23 Pierre Ponsot, 'Les rendements des céréales en Basse-Andalousie du XVIIe au XIXe siècle', *Actes du Colloque préparatoire* (forthcoming).

24 R. Kain, 'Les dîmes, les relevés de dîmes et la mesure de la production agricole dans la Grande-Bretagne préindustrielle', *Actes du Colloque préparatoire* (forthcoming).

3. Methodology

1 Certain tithes are known to have been levied after the French Revolution and to have survived for several decades of the nineteenth century. See especially A. Soboul, *Problèmes paysans de la Révolution, 1789–1848*, Paris, 1976, Chapter 7: 'Survivances féodales dans la société rurale du XIXe siècle', also published in *Annales E.S.C.* (1958); Serge Abadam, 'La Révolution et les luttes des métayers', *Etudes Rurales* 59 (1975); Rives (1976).

2 See below, p. 43ff., especially 49.

3 See E. Le Roy Ladurie and B. Veyrasset-Herren, 'La rente foncière autour de Paris au XVIIe siècle', *Annales E.S.C.* (1968); J. P. Desaive, 'A la recherche d'un indicateur de la conjoncture. Baux de Notre Dame de Paris et de l'abbaye de Montmartre' in Goy and Le Roy Ladurie (1972).

4 M. T. Lorcin, 'Un musée imaginaire de la ruse paysanne: la fraude des décimables du XIVe au XVIIIe siècle dans la région lyonnaise', *Etudes Rurales* 5 (1973); id. 'La fraude des décimables: mouvement court ou mouvement long?' in *Actes du Colloque préparatoire* (forthcoming).

5 J. Rives, *Dîme et société dans l'Archevêché d'Auch au XVIIIe siècle*, Paris, 1976.

6 Nicolas (1978); id. 'L'enjeu décimal dans l'espace rural savoyard', in *Actes du Colloque préparatoire* (forthcoming).

7 Morineau (1970), 21–2.

8 G. Frêche, 'Dîme et production agricole. Remarques méthodologiques à propos de la région toulousaine' in Goy and Le Roy Ladurie (1972); Frêche (1974), 519ff.

9 M. Morineau, 'Réflexions tardives et conclusions prospectives' in Goy and Le Roy Ladurie (1972), 321.

10 J. Goy, 'Dîmes, rendements, état des récoltes et revenu agricole réel', *Studi Storici* (1968); id. 'Les rendements du blé en pays d'Arles, XVIIe–XVIIIIe siècles' in Goy and Le Roy Ladurie (1972), 245. Another article on yield ratios derived from four farms in Arles is in press; it was given as a paper at Prato.

11 See Appendix to Chapter 1.

12 Frêche (1974), 215.

13 Rives (1976), 13–14.

14 Rives (1976), 41ff.

15 Rives (1976), 144. My italics.

16 It remains to be shown (despite Georges Frêche's thesis and the book by Jean Rives), that there is any considerable discrepancy between the tithe curves and possible data concerning the gross agricultural product.

17 Goy and Le Roy Ladurie (1972), 374.

18 Lemeunier (1975), 361.

19 Guy Lemeunier, 'Approche méthodologique des dîmes de Murcie (Espagne) à l'époque moderne', in *Actes du Colloque préparatoire* (forthcoming).

20 J. Goy, 'Dîmes, rendements, état des récoltes et revenu agricole réel', *Studi Storici* (1968); Baehrel (1961); Morineau (1970) and the Spanish, Belgian and Hungarian studies already mentioned.

21 J. Goy and A. L. Head-Koenig, 'Une expérience. Les revenus décimaux en France méditerranéenne, XVIe–XVIIIe siècles', *Etudes Rurales* 36 (1969) and also Goy and Le Roy Ladurie (1972), 255ff.

22 B. Garnier, 'Pays herbagers, pays céréaliers et pays ouverts en Normandie (XVIe–début XIXe siècle)', *Revue d'histoire économique et sociale* (1975).

23 Neveux (1980); id. 'La production céréalière dans une région frontalière: le Cambrésis du XVe au XVIIIe siècles. Bilan provisoire', in Goy and Le Roy Ladurie (1972), 58ff.

24 See the first 235 pages of Neveux (1980) for details of the method used.

25 See Neveux (1980), 196ff. on this topic; see also the comments of Morineau in 'Cambrésis et Hainaut: des frères ennemis?' in *Actes du Colloque préparatoire* (forthcoming).

26 *Economics. An Introductory Analysis*, New York, 1967.

27 Le Roy Ladurie (1966), 228.

28 Goy and Head-Koenig (1969), 255ff. See also J. Goy, 'Las fluctuaciones del producto del diezmo en Francia mediterranea (siglos XVI–XVIII)', *Desarollo economico* 36 (1970).

29 Le Roy Ladurie (1966), G 23.

30 *Les prix des grains, des vins et légumes à Toulouse, 1386–1868*, Paris, 1967, pp. 85ff.

31 Ibid. Chapter 5.

32 Ernest Labrousse's phrase.

33 A. Eiras Roel, 'Dîme et mouvement du produit agricole en Galicie (1600–1837)' in *Actes du Colloque préparatoire* (forthcoming).

34 Goy and Le Roy Ladurie (1972), 321ff. and especially p. 328.

35 G. Paquet and J. P. Wallot, 'Rentes foncières, dîmes et revenus paysans: le cas canadien' in *Actes du Colloque préparatoire* (forthcoming).

36 M. Baulant, 'Du bon usage des dîmes dans la région parisienne' in *Actes du Colloque préparatoire* (forthcoming).

37 See references in n.3 above and also the following papers in Goy and Le Roy Ladurie (1972): J. P. Desaive, 'A la recherche d'un indicateur de la conjoncture. Baux de Notre Dame de Paris et de l'abbaye de Montmartre'; A. L. Head-Koenig, 'Rente foncière et dîmes dans le Lyonnais au XVIIe et XVIIIe siècles: leur concordance'; G. Gangneux, 'Les rentes seigneuriales et domaniales dans les Commanderies de l'Ordre de Malte de la Langue de Provence, XVIIe–XVIIIe siècles'.

38 See Appendix to Chapter 1 for the contents of the *Actes du Colloque préparatoire* (forthcoming).

39 Hermann Van der Wee had already raised some novel problems in his book *The Growth of the Antwerp Market and the European Economy*, The Hague, 1963.

40 J. Jacquart, 'La rente foncière, indice conjectural?' *Revue Historique* 514 (1975).

41 For the copious bibliography on ground rents, see the article by Jacquart cited in the previous note and also vol. II of Braudel and Labrousse (1970) and Neveux *et al.* (1975).
See also the article 'Problèmes agraires et société rurale. Normandie et Europe du Nord-Ouest, XIVe–XIXe siècles', *Cahiers des Annales de Normandie* 11.

42 See previous note for references.

43 See Appendix to Chapter 1.

44 Slicher Van Bath, *The Agrarian History of Western Europe*, London, 1959, and *Yield Ratios*, A.A.G.B. 10, Wageningen, 1963; J. Z. Titow, *Winchester Yields. A Study in Medieval Agricultural Productivity*, Cambridge, 1972.

45 M. Aymard, 'En Sicile. Dîmes et comptabilités agricoles' in Goy and Le Roy Ladurie (1972), 294ff.

46 'La mesure de la production et des rendements céréaliers en Allemagne et en Suisse à l'époque moderne' in *Proceedings* 1.

47 P. Ponsot, 'Rendement des céréales et rente foncière dans la Campina de Cordoue (début XVIe–début XIXe)', *Cuadernos de Historia* 7 (1977).

48 J. Goy (forthcoming, see n.10 above).

49 *Revue d'histoire économique et sociale* 2–3 (1975).

50 *La formation des prix céréaliers en Brabant et en Flandre au XVe siècle*, Brussels, 1975.

51 H. Neveux and M.-J.Tits-Dieuaide, 'Etude structurelle des fluctuations courtes des rendements céréaliers dans l'Europe du Nord-Ouest (XIVe–XVIe siècles)', *Cahiers des Annales de Normandie* 11 (1979).

52 See the article by Neveux previously cited (n.23) and also that by Neveux and M.-J. Tits-Dieuaide in *Historische Sozialwissenschaftliche Forschungen* 4 (1978).

53 See Appendix to Chapter 1 and *Proceedings* 1.

4. Towards another kind of history

1 See B. Garnier, 'Dîme et production agricole au XVIIIe siècle. Une source inexploitée: les déclarations des revenues des curés', *Annales de Normandie* (1973).

2 J. Revel, 'Rendements, production et productivité: les grands domaines de la Campagne romaine aux XVIIe et XVIIIe siècles' in *Actes du Colloque préparatoire* (forthcoming).

3 'Les productions animales et végétales dans les montagnes d'Auvergne au XVIIIe siècle' in *Actes du Colloque préparatoire* (forthcoming).

4 See particularly J. Nicolas, 'Le problème des dîmes en Savoie à la veille de la Révolution' in *Actes du 89e Congrès national des Sociétés Savantes*, Lyon, 1964; Nicolas (1978), 676ff.; 'La dîme, contrats d'affermages et autres documents décimaux' in *La pratique des documents anciens* (multiple authorship), Annecy, 1978; 'L'enjeu décimal dans l'espace rural savoyard' in *Actes du Colloque préparatoire* (forthcoming).

5 Nicolas (1978), 749–60.

5. The end of the Middle Ages

1 Goy and Le Roy Ladurie (1972).
2 Baehrel (1961).
3 See above, pp. 16, 44–5.
4 Neveux (1980).
5 Bois (1976); H. Neveux, J. Jacquart and E. Le Roy Ladurie, *Histoire de la France rurale*, vol. II: *L'Age classique des paysans*, Paris, 1975.
6 Braudel and Labrousse (1970), vol. 1, part 2.
7 M. M. Postan, *The Medieval Economy and Society*, London, 1972.
8 Bois (1976), 304–7.
9 Bois (1976).
10 Bois (1976), 313.
11 Morineau (1970).
12 Morineau (1970), 7–23.

6. The recovery of the sixteenth century

1 Le Roy Ladurie (1966), especially the chapter on wages.
2 'Les fluctuations de la production agricole en Pologne aux XVIe–XVIIe siècles' in *Actes du Colloque préparatoire* (forthcoming).
3 See Appendix to Chapter 1; papers to be published in *Actes du Colloque préparatoire* (forthcoming).
4 'Productivité, évolution du prix d'affermage et superficie de l'entreprise agricole aux Pays-Bas du XIVe au XVIIIe siècle' in *Actes du Colloque préparatoire* (forthcoming).
5 Van der Wee (1978), 2.
6 M.-J. Tits-Dieuaide, 'Cereal Yields around Louvain, 1404–1726', in Van der Wee (1978), 99.
7 Van der Wee (1978), 11.
8 M.-J. Tits-Dieuaide, 'Peasant Dues in Brabant. The Example of the Meldert Farm near Tirlemont, 1380–1797', in Van der Wee (1978), 114.
9 Frêche (1974).
10 R. Brenner, 'Agrarian Class Structure and Economic Development in Preindustrial Europe', *Past and Present* 70 (1976).
11 Coleman, *The Economy of England, 1450–1750*, London, 1977.
12 G. Fourquin, *Les campagnes de la région parisienne à la fin du*

moyen âge, Paris, 1963, *in fine*; Bois (1976).

13 On the Beauce, see J. M. Constant, 'L'evolution de la rente foncière et de la rentabilité de la terre en Beauce aux XVIe et XVIIe siècles' in *Actes du Colloque préparatoire* (forthcoming).

14 On Switzerland, see A. L. Head-Koenig, 'Les fluctuations des rendements et du produit décimal céréaliers dans quelques régions du plateau suisse, 1560–1800' in *Actes du Colloque préparatoire* (forthcoming).

15 M. Baulant, 'Le salaire des ouvriers du bâtiment à Paris de 1400 à 1726', *Annales E.S.C.* 26 (1971).

16 Joan Thirsk (personal communication).

17 Braudel and Labrousse (1970), 583.

18 G. de Gouberville, *Journal*, Caen, 1892.

19 Jacquart (1974).

20 G. Anes Alvarez, 'Las fluctuaciones de la producción agricola durante el siglo XVIII y comienzos del XIX en Espana' in *Actes du Colloque préparatoire* (forthcoming).

21 L. M. Bilbao and E. F. de Pinedo, 'Evolución del producto agricola bruto en el Pais Vasco peninsular, 1537–1850. Primeira aproximación a traves de los diezmos y de la primacia' in *Actes du Colloque préparatoire* (forthcoming).

22 Anes Alvarez (n. 20).

23 Bilbao and de Pinedo (n. 21).

24 M. Aymard, 'Production et productivités agricoles: l'Italie du Sud à l'époque moderne' in *Actes du Colloque préparatoire* (forthcoming).

25 Aymard (n. 24).

26 Aymard (n. 24).

27 Aymard (n. 24).

28 Braudel and Labrousse (1970).

7. The seventeenth century

1 M. Morineau, 'La crise du XVIIe siècle', *Actes du VIIIe Colloque de Marseille* (1978).

2 L. Makkai *et al*, 'Les registres de dîme comme sources de l'histoire de la production agricole en Hongrie dans la période du féodalisme tardif, 1500–1848' in *Actes du Colloque préparatoire* (forthcoming).

3 See Appendix to Chapter 1 for the paper by Topolski and Wyczanski.

4 E. Le Roy Ladurie, 'L'histoire immobile' in Le Roy Ladurie (1978).

5 C. Carrière, *Negociants marseillais au XVIIIe siècle*, Marseille, 1973; J. Delumeau, *Le mouvement du port de Saint-Malo, 1681–1720*, Rennes, 1966.

6 J. Garnier, 'Elements de conjoncture: production et rente foncière en Normandie, Maine et Anjou' in *Actes du Colloque préparatoire* (forthcoming).

7   Bois (1976).
8   Van der Wee (1978).
9   Braudel and Labrousse (1970), 270.
10 Van der Wee (1978), 13.
11 Braudel and Labrousse (1970), 780.
12 Braudel and Labrousse (1970), 763.
13 Garnier (n. 6).
14 Phase B is a long-term period (30–40 or 100 years) when prices are stagnating, declining or consistently at a low level.
15 See Appendix to Chapter 1 for these papers, to appear in *Actes du Colloque préparatoire*.
16 A. L. Head-Koenig (see Appendix to Chapter 1); see Figure 7.
17 Braudel and Labrousse (1970), 773–4 and 784.
18 See Jean Meuvret, *Etudes d'histoire économique*, Paris, 1971, and Goubert (1960).
19 E. Appolis, *Le diocèse civil de Lodève*, Albi, 1951.
20 See Le Roy Ladurie's contributions to Braudel and Labrousse (1970).
21 See Garnier, *Actes du Colloque préparatoire* (forthcoming).
22 A. D. Wrigley, 'A Simple Model of London's Importance, 1650–1750', *Past and Present* 37 (1967).
23 Garnier, *Actes du Colloque préparatoire* (forthcoming).
24 Van der Wee (1978), 14.
25 Van der Wee (1978), 15.
26 Ibid.
27 Delille (1973).
28 Aymard, *Actes du Colloque préparatoire* (forthcoming).
29 Delille (1973).
30 Aymard (n. 28).
31 Papers by Aymard and Basini, *Actes du Colloque préparatoire* (forthcoming).
32 G. Anes Alvarez, *Actes du Colloque préparatoire* (forthcoming); Jacquart (1974).
33 Vilar (1962).
34 G. Lemeunier, *Actes du Colloque préparatoire* (forthcoming).
35 A. Eiras Roel, *Actes du Colloque préparatoire* (forthcoming).
36 L. M. Bilbao and E. F. de Pinedo, *Actes du Colloque préparatoire* (forthcoming).
37 Coleman (1977); see also E. A. Wrigley and R. S. Schofield, *The Population History of England 1541–1871: A Reconstruction*, London, 1981.
38 Morineau (n.1).

8. The eighteenth century

1   See the papers by Makkai *et al* and by Kiss in *Actes du Colloque préparatoire* (forthcoming).
2   These figures have been obtained by dividing 1.3 million tons (the

rye, wheat and barley produced in 1570) by 3.4 million inhabitants; and 1,174,000 tons by 4.5 million inhabitants for 1789. On Poland, see the papers by Topolski and Wyczanski in *Actes du Colloque préparatoire.*

3 P. Deane and W. Cole, *British Economic Growth*, Cambridge, 1962, and the summary in Coleman (1977).

4 E. A. Wrigley and R. S. Schofield, *The Population History of England 1541–1871: A Reconstruction*, London, 1981.

5 Deane and Cole (n.3), 65.

6 D. Dickson, 'Tithe and rent as sources for Irish agricultural trends before 1815', *Actes du Colloque préparatoire* (forthcoming).

7 Van der Wee (1978).

8 By 'Holland' and 'Belgium' I mean the territories now occupied by the states of those names.

9 Van der Wee (1978), 180.

10 Basini, *Actes du Colloque préparatoire* (forthcoming).

11 Ibid.

12 On Apulia, see M. A. Visceglia, 'Rente féodale et agriculture dans Les Pouilles à l'époque moderne, XVIe–XVIIIe siècles', *Actes du Colloque préparatoire* (forthcoming); cf. Vilar (1962).

13 Information kindly given orally by C. Poni.

14 Aymard, *Actes du Colloque préparatoire* (forthcoming).

15 J. Revel, *Actes du Colloque préparatoire* (forthcoming).

16 P. Macry, *Marché, société et commerce du grain à Naples*, Naples, 1974.

17 J. Georgelin, *Venise au Siècle des Lumières*, Paris/The Hague, 1978.

18 F. Landi, 'Il frumento nell'economia ravennate', *Mélanges de l'Ecole Française de Rome* 11 (1976).

19 Review of L. Valensi, *Fellahs tunisiens (18e–19e siècles)* in *L'Histoire* (6 November 1978).

20 G. Anes Alvarez in *Proceedings* (see above, p. 7): What follows owes an enormous amount to the work of Anes Alvarez, and, of course, to the other Spanish historians who have written monographs on particular regions.

21 Anes Alvarez, *Proceedings* II, 548.

22 P. Ponsot, *Actes du Colloque préparatoire* (forthcoming).

23 Anes Alvarez, *Actes du Colloque préparatoire* (forthcoming).

24 M. Carmagnani in Goy and Le Roy Ladurie (1972).

25 A. de Araujo Oliveira, 'Prestations paysannes, dîmes, rente foncière et mouvement de la production agricole à l'époque préindustrielle dans le pays du Nord-Ouest portugais', *Actes du Colloque préparatoire* (forthcoming).

26 Deane and Cole (n. 3).

27 Neveux *et al* (1975), 395; Goy and Le Roy Ladurie (1972), 370.

28 E. Le Roy Ladurie, 'The chief defects of Gregory King' in Le Roy Ladurie (1978). King was not well informed about France.

29 Goy and Le Roy Ladurie (1972), 373.

30 M. Baulant in Goy and Le Roy Ladurie (1972).
31 Ibid.
32 Le Roy Ladurie (1966).
33 See Bernard Derouet's unpublished doctoral thesis on 'Villages du Thimerais au XVIIIe siècle. Essai de démographie sociale differentielle et d'économie historique' for the University of Paris, 1978. See also his article 'Une démographie sociale differentielle: Clés pour un système auto-régulateur des populations d'Ancien Régime', *Annales E.S.C.* 35 (Jan/Feb 1980), 3–41.
34 See the papers by Pavard, Garnier and Tits-Dieuaide in *Actes du Colloque préparatoire* (forthcoming).
35 Ibid.
36 J. P. Perrot, *Genèse d'une ville moderne: Caen au XVIIIe siècle*, 2 vols., Paris/The Hague, 1975.
37 Garnier, *Actes du Colloque préparatoire*.
38 Ibid.
39 P. Chaunu, 'Reflexions sur la démographie normande', *Hommages à Marcel Reinhard*, Paris, 1973, p. 105.
40 These percentages have been calculated by Mme Tits from Gangneux's data.
41 Frêche (1974); cf. Goy and Le Roy Ladurie (1972), 222, and M. T. Lorcin's paper in *Actes du Colloque préparatoire* (forthcoming).
42 L. Gangneux, *Actes du Colloque préparatoire* (forthcoming).
43 T. Le Goff, *Actes du Colloque préparatoire* (forthcoming). The adjective 'fairly good' refers to seventeenth-century Brittany purely from an agricultural point of view; the revolt of 1675 clearly expressed malaise.
44 Goubert in Braudel and Labrousse (1970).
45 Goubert (1960).
46 See the papers by J. Garnier (Maine and Anjou) and C. Chereau (Maine) in *Actes du Colloque préparatoire* (forthcoming).
47 Nicolas (1978); A. M. Piuz, 'Marché de la viande à Genève', *Annales E.S.C.* (1975).
48 See the unpublished thesis by A. Molinier on the history of Vivarais from the sixteenth to the eighteenth century.
49 A. L. Head-Koenig, *Actes du Colloque préparatoire* (forthcoming).
50 Piuz (n.47).
51 U. Braker, *Le pauvre homme du Toggenbourg*, Lausanne, 1978, a peasant autobiography.

References

Baehrel (1961). R. Baehrel, *Une croissance. La Basse-Provence rurale (fin du XVIe siècle – 1789)*, Paris.

Bois (1976). G. Bois, *Crise du féodalisme. Economie rurale et démographie en Normandie orientale au début du XVIe siècle*, Paris.

Braudel and Labrousse (1970). F. Braudel and C. E. Labrousse (eds.), *Histoire économique et sociale de la France*, Vol. I, part 2, Paris.

Carmagnani (1973). M. Carmagnani, *Les mécanismes de la vie économique dans une société coloniale: le Chili (1680–1830)*, Paris.

Coleman (1977). D. C. Coleman, *The Economy of England, 1450–1750*, London.

Delille (1973). G. Delille, *Croissance d'une société rurale*, Naples.

Deyon (n.d.). P. Deyon, *Contribution a l'étude des revenus fonciers en Picardie. Les fermages de l'Hôtel-Dieu d'Amiens et leurs variations de 1515 à 1789*, Lille.

Frêche (1974). G. Frêche, *Toulouse et la région Midi-Pyrenées au Siècle des Lumières, vers 1670–1789*, Paris.

Garnier (1975). B. Garnier, 'Pays herbagers, pays céréaliers et pays ouverts en Normandie (XVIe-début XIXe siècle)', *Revue d'histoire économique et sociale*.

Goubert (1960). P. Goubert, *Beauvais et le Beauvaisis de 1600 à 1730*, Paris.

Goy and Head-Koenig (1969). J. Goy and A. L. Head-Koenig, 'Une expérience. Les revenus décimaux en France méditerranéenne, XVIe-XVIIIe siècles', *Etudes Rurales 36*.

Goy and Le Roy Ladurie (1972). J. Goy and E. Le Roy Ladurie (eds.), *Les fluctuations du produit de la dîme. Conjoncture décimale et domaniale de la fin du Moyen-Age au XVIIIe siècle*, Paris.

Jacquart (1974). J. Jacquart, *La crise rurale en Ile-de-France, 1550–1670*, Paris.

Le Roy Ladurie (1966). E. Le Roy Ladurie, *Les paysans de Languedoc*, Paris; 2nd ed., 1974; abridged ed. (same title), 1969; English ed. (*Peasants of Languedoc*), Urbana, Ill., 1974.

Le Roy Ladurie (1978). E. Le Roy Ladurie, *Le territoire de l'historien*, vol. II, Paris; English ed. (*The Territory of the Historian*), Hassocks, 1979.

Lemeunier (1975). G. Lemeunier, *La part de Dieu*, Mélanges de la Casa de Velasquez XI, Madrid.

References

Morineau (1970). M. Morineau, *Les faux-semblants d'un démarrage économique: agriculture et démographie en France au XVIIIe siècle*, Paris.

Neveux (1980). H. Neveux, *Les grains du Cambrésis (fin du XIVe–début du XVIIe siècles). Vie et déclin d'une structure économique*, Paris.

Neveux *et al* (1975). H. Neveux, J. Jacquart and E. Le Roy Ladurie, *Histoire de la France rurale*, Vol. II, Paris.

Nicolas (1978). J. Nicolas, *La Savoie au XVIIIe siècle. Noblesse et bourgeoisie*, Paris.

Poitrineau (1965). A. Poitrineau, *La vie rurale en Basse-Auvergne au XVIIIe siècle (1726–1789)*, Paris.

Proceedings. M. Flinn (ed.), *Proceedings of the Seventh International Economic History Congress*, Edinburgh, 1978.

Rives (1976). J. Rives, *Dîme et société dans l'Archevêché d'Auch au XVIIIe siècle*, Paris.

Van der Wee (1978). H. Van der Wee and E. van Cauwenberghe, *Productivity of Land and Agricultural Innovation in the Low Countries (1250–1800)*, Louvain.

Verhulst and Vandenbroecke (1979). A. Verhulst and C. Vandenbroecke (eds.), *Landbouwproduktiviteit in Vlaanderen en Brabant 14de – 18de eeuw.*, Ghent.

Vilar (1962). P. Vilar, *La Catalogne dans l'Espagne moderne*, Paris.

Actes du Colloque préparatoire. Papers presented at the 1977 conference in Paris in preparation for the Seventh International Economic History Congress. The titles of the papers, arranged geographically, are printed as the Appendix to Chapter 1.

Marianne into Battle

Republican Imagery and Symbolism in France, 1789–1880

MAURICE AGULHON

Since the French Revolution the allegorical figure variously known as 'France', 'the Republic', or 'Marianne', has had a dual role as a visual image of the nation and as the symbol of the French Republic as a specific political regime. In this volume Professor Agulhon draws on the works of artists and writers, and also on the many manifestations of popular culture in prints, cartoons and songs, in an analysis which shows how the eventful political history of nineteenth-century France is reflected in an equally complex history of the visual representation of the Republican regime and ideal.

Available in hard covers and as a paperback

Interpreting the French Revolution

FRANÇOIS FURET

The French Revolution is an historical event unlike any other. It is more than just a topic of intellectual interest: it has become part of a moral and political heritage. But even after two centuries this central event in French history has usually been thought of in much the same terms as it was by its contemporaries. This book is an attempt to cut through the contradictory and misleading views of the Revolution, and to decipher some of the enigmatic problems of revolutionary ideology. Professor Furet analyses how such an event can be conceptualised, and identifies the radical changes the revolution produced as well as the continuity it provided, albeit under the appearance of change.

Available in hard covers and as a paperback

Industrialization before Industrialization
Rural Industry in the Genesis of Capitalism
PETER KRIEDTE, HANS MEDICK
and JÜRGEN SCHLUMBOHM

Beginning in the late middle ages, and accelerating in the sixteenth and seventeenth centuries, there developed in many rural regions of Europe a domestic industry, mass-producing craft goods for distant markets. This book presents an analysis of this 'proto-industrialization' and considers whether it constituted a distinct mode of production, different from the preceding feudal economy and from subsequent industrial capitalism, or was part of a process of continuous evolution characterised by the spread of wage labour and the penetration of capitalism into the process of production.

Studies in Modern Capitalism/Etudes sur le Capitalisme Moderne
and *Past and Present Publications*
Available in hard covers and as a paperback

Economic Life in Ottoman Europe
Taxation, Trade and the Struggle for Land, 1600–1800
BRUCE McGOWAN

Historians of the southeastern European lands once ruled by the Ottomans have been severely hampered by a lack of information about the economic life of the area in the period prior to the nineteenth century. In this book, Bruce McGowan presents original new material concerning this neglected field. He provides convincing analyses of economic, fiscal, and demographic questions fundamental to our understanding of these lands, and offers valuable data for the continuing study of the role of Ottoman Europe within the expanding economy of the early modern centuries.

Studies in Modern Capitalism/Etudes sur le Capitalisme Moderne

The European Periphery and Industrialization, 1780–1914
IVÁN T. BEREND and GYÖRGY RÁNKI

The swift progress of the 'European core' during the first half of the nineteenth century created a distinction within Europe between advanced and underdeveloped nations which in many ways parallels, and sheds light on, the worldwide North–South dialogue today. While emphasis is placed on economic factors in this examination of the nature of underdevelopment in the European 'periphery', the social and political aspects of the core/periphery distinction are also taken into account.

Studies in Modern Capitalism/Etudes sur le Capitalisme Moderne